# Early
# Flemish
## Painting

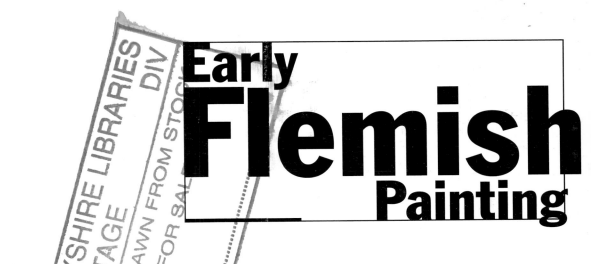

# Early Flemish Painting

Jean-Claude Frère

·TERRAIL·

Editors: Jean-Claude Dubost and Jean-François Gonthier
Cover design: Gérard Lo Monaco and Laurent Gudin
Art Director: Marthe Lauffray
Editorial Supervision: Aude Simon
Editorial Assistant: Claire Néollier
English Translation: Peter Snowdon
Picture Research: Nathalie Bréaud
Typesetting and Filmsetting: D.V. Arts Graphiques, 28000 Chartres
Lithography: Litho Service T. Zamboni, Verona

© FINEST SA/ÉDITIONS TERRAIL, PARIS 1997
The Art Book Subsidiary
of BAYARD PRESSE SA
ISBN 2-87939-120-2
Publication number: 135
Printed in Italy.

# CONTENTS

# FLANDERS UNDER THE DUKES OF BURGUNDY

Every year, three hundred thousand people visit the hôtel-Dieu in Beaune and pause in front of Rogier Van der Weyden's polyptych, *The Last Judgement.* Yet how many of them stop to wonder why they are looking at a work by a Flemish master, rather than a local artist? And how many of them make the connection between this apparent anomaly and the Broederlam altarpiece, which is one of the treasures of the musée des Beaux-Arts in Dijon? Broederlam too came from Flanders, but he painted his single surviving work for the nearby chartreuse de Champmol. Philip the Bold had founded the monastery to serve as a vast funerary monument to himself and his descendants, just as the basilica of St Denis had been built to immortalize and consecrate the royal house of France. Besides Broederlam's altarpiece, the Dijon museum also contains yet another masterpiece by a leading figure of the golden age of Flemish painting, Robert Campin's *Nativity.* How did these three works, which we would not have been surprised to find in Ghent, Bruges or Antwerp, come to be concentrated in one small corner of north-eastern France?

The answer is simple. In the 15th and 16th centuries, the small wine-growing region that we know today as Burgundy was the heartland of a powerful and extensive state. Its territories lay sandwiched between the Kingdom of France and the Holy Roman Empire, and stretched as far afield as Flanders and Brabant.

The Duchy of Burgundy had its heyday under Philip the Bold, John the Fearless, Philip the Good and Charles the Bold. Between them, they acquired countless new territories, through a cunning combination of astute marriages, timely purchase and the barely legal diversion of other people's inheritances. As a result, they came to rule over a State whose subjects had various origins and spoke different languages. Although it was not geographically continuous, and therefore particularly vulnerable to attack by hostile forces, the Burgundian empire was chiefly made up of densely populated urban areas, which provided the foundation for its military strength and commercial prosperity. By the middle of the 15th century, the province of Flanders alone had seven hundred thousand inhabitants, a third of whom were city-dwellers. Such

*Above*
HIERONYMUS BOSCH
*The Temptation of St Anthony*
Detail.
Museo del Prado, Madrid.

*Opposite*
ROGIER VAN DER WEYDEN
*Portrait of Philip the Good*
After 1450, oil on wood, 31×23 cm (12×9 in).
Kunsthistorisches Museum, Vienna.

*Left*
DIERIC BOUTS
*The Fall*
Detail.
Musée des Beaux-Arts, Lille.

a concentration of population in cities was unprecedented in Europe at that time. The Duke's large court was notoriously flamboyant and spared no expense on lavish entertainments. The towns were thronged with craftsmen who traded throughout the entire world. The ports could barely cope with the volume of goods that flowed both in and out. Under the Dukes of Burgundy, Flanders rapidly developed into a hotbed of artistic activity whose only serious European rival was Northern Italy.

In that society, painters occupied an especially privileged position. There was a highly developed system of patronage led by the clergy, who had long understood the power of imagery. Their example was followed by princes and municipalities, who sought to bend art to their political aims. The same artists and craftsmen who worked for the princes and prelates would also receive commissions from aristocrats, civil servants and magistrates, as well as from merchants, both from Flanders and from further afield. In this way, those lower down the social hierarchy could imagine they were a little closer to their rulers, whose fabulous way of life they could not hope to emulate. The diversity of Jan Van Eyck's clients was quite typical in this respect: they included, as well as the Burgundian court, Josse Vidj, a burgher of Ghent, Canon Georges Van der Paele of Bruges, and Giovanni Arnolfini, an Italian merchant and banker. The list of Rogier Van der Weyden's commissions reveals a similar heterogeneity, ranging from the city of Brussels and the court of Burgundy, to Nicolas Rolin, chancellor of Burgundy, Pierre Bladelin, Philip the Good's chief treasurer, and Jean Gros, first secretary to Charles the Bold. Art was intimately bound up with new patterns of social mobility, and an artist who refused to bow to the prevailing conventions could not always rely upon finding patronage, as Robert Campin discovered.

In those days, artists did not work alone, as they do now. A successful painter would be in charge of a studio, which he would run like a small business, promoting its reputation, pursuing commissions and fighting off competition. From the rules laid down by the guilds, we can glean that a typical master's premises would include a home for his family and his workers, a studio, and a shop, or at least some sort of window where he could display work for sale. Like all craftsmen, he would employ workers of varying levels of skill and experience. Most of the men who worked for him were either apprentices, whom he would house and feed for a fixed period, usually four years, or fellow guild-members, who had already completed their training. Paintings were essentially collective productions, and it was not uncommon for two masters to sign a contract together, or to share a studio. As a result, the parentage of most Flemish paintings of that period is inextricably mixed, and the attribution of particular works can be highly problematic.

Early Flemish painting was, in many ways, a modernizing art. It was certainly the only major school of painting in Europe at that time. Elsewhere, however, a revolution was in the offing. In Florence, central

*Above and left*
HIERONYMUS BOSCH
*Triptych*
*The Last Judgement*
Left wing, details of
*Adam and Eve expelled*
*from Paradise.*
Akademie der Bildenden
Kuenste, Vienna.

perspective was soon to be discovered by Brunelleschi, in around 1420. In 1435, the new system was codified by Alberti. Central perspective was founded on Euclidean geometry, the reduction of space to a grid, and the establishment of a single vanishing point at the horizon. Mathematical calculation had, apparently, revealed that the universe was governed by a system of lines. This analytical approach stood in stark contrast to that of the Flemish artists, whose perspective was, to begin with, an entirely empirical process. To construct their picture space, they would use several zones of convergence, each with its own distinct vanishing point. They were particularly fond of setting their subject in a shallow architectural cube, within which they would place convex circular mirrors. (Examples of this practice can be seen in the paintings of Jan Van Eyck and Quentin Massys.) These mirrors would gather and reflect dimensions of their surroundings that would otherwise go unseen, thus projecting and multiplying depth in complex ways.

*Above and left*
HIERONYMUS BOSCH
*Triptych*
*The Last Judgement*
Left wing, details of
*Adam and Eve expelled*
*from Paradise.*
Akademie der Bildenden
Kuenste, Vienna.

The most original feature of Flemish art in that period, however, was not its method of spatial representation, but its use of oil-based paint. This medium seems to have been familiar and employed in Ancient Rome. But the Flemish masters were the first to generalize its use, by inventing new binders which made it easier to handle. When Flemish painters first travelled to Italy, they astonished both artists and art lovers not so much by the profound spiritual integrity of their work, but rather by the tiny details which their new technique made possible. The application of fresh oil paint to a dry surface enabled both to correct one's first ideas and to superimpose different tones. It was this technical advance which lay behind the extraordinary flowering of the art of portraiture in Burgundian Flanders. No other school of painters had yet portrayed the face as the mirror of the mind with such precision, or modelled the contours of the flesh so accurately.

We might look in vain for any greater artistic unity encompassing the work that was produced throughout the lands that lie between Antwerp and Dijon. Burgundian art was dominated by the art of Flanders. Yet it was the wealth and power of the "foreign" State by whom they were ruled that provided Flemish painters with the market and the patrons they needed in order to flourish. In discussing their work in this book, I have chosen to proceed chronologically, tracing the development of Flemish painting over three generations. A thematic analysis would have led to an undue amount of repetition, since themes were not usually selected by the artists themselves, but imposed by their clients. Unfortunately, only approximate dates of birth and death of most of these painters can be given, on the basis of detective work carried out in various archives. Unlike the artists of the Italian Renaissance, the painters of Flanders were not lucky enough to find their Vasari, and we have therefore dispose of no comprehensive contemporary record of their lives.

# THE ORIGINS OF FLEMISH ART

The dawn of the 15th century saw the beginning of a new era in Flemish art. In 1399, an altarpiece painted by Melchior Broederlam was delivered to the town of Dijon. This work defines the moment at which the technique of illumination, the finest exponents of which were the Limbourg brothers, yielded its supremacy to the art of painting on wooden panels. Miniaturists were no longer in the vanguard. Their place had been taken by a new breed of artist – the painter.

Broederlam's Dijon altarpiece was the first fruit of this new art, and the first work to embody a new set of conventions. His style derived from the International Gothic style. It was imbued with a natural elegance and refinement, and its rich textures can be seen as the pictorial equivalent of the values of the European aristocracy. It was a large-scale art, that rose to the challenge inherent in its dimensions; but above all, it entirely superseded the essentially decorative approach of the miniaturists. Miniature work, by its very size, could only incorporate a few isolated details. Henceforth the subjects of art, although still predominantly sacred, would be approached in a comprehensively realistic manner. Painting was to be an art firmly rooted in the world. A pictorial revolution was born.

MELCHIOR BROEDERLAM
*Dijon Altarpiece*
Detail of right wing,
*The Flight into Egypt.*
Musée des Beaux-Arts, Dijon.

# MELCHIOR BROEDERLAM

Melchior Broederlam was probably born in Ypres although we possess no clues as to the dates of his birth and death, or what training he may have had. The little we do know of him relates entirely to his activity as a court painter between 1381 and 1410.

Broederlam was appointed an official painter some time before 1381. He worked initially for Louis de Mäle, Count of Flanders, and subsequently for his son-in-law, Philip the Bold, Duke of Burgundy. The accounts of the Duchy's payroll show that Broederlam received fees on various occasions for painting banners, chairs, coats of arms and escutcheons. He was also responsible for decorating the flagship of the Duke's fleet. In the course of his service to Philip, he travelled to Lille – where he painted extensive murals for the château de Hesdin – and to Paris and Dijon. Yet, although his commissions involved him in journeys throughout the territories of Burgundy and France, Broederlam nevertheless continued to reside in the town where he was born.

In 1407, he painted portraits of the Duke of Burgundy and his wife for the chapel of the Counts of Courtrai. At the request of Philip the Bold, he also painted both the outer panels and inner polychrome decoration of at least two altarpieces sculpted by Jacques de Baerze, that were intended for the chartreuse de champmol. The chartreuse had been built by Philip to serve as a funerary monument to his dynasty.

Of these two altarpieces, only that in the musée des Beaux-Arts in Dijon still features its painted outer panels. Although we know from information in the Ducal archives that Broederlam worked in Dijon from 1393 to 1399, the two panels which make up this work are the only fragment of his œuvre to have survived down to the present day. Between them, they represent four biblical scenes: on the left, *The Annunciation* and

*Above*
MELCHIOR BROEDERLAM
*Dijon Altarpiece*
Detail of left wing,
*The Visitation.*
Musée des Beaux-Arts, Dijon.

*Opposite*
*Dijon Altarpiece*
Detail of left wing,
*The Annunciation.*

MELCHIOR BROEDERLAM
*Dijon Altarpiece*
1393-1399, tempera on wood,
165.5×249 cm (65×98 in).
Musée des Beaux-Arts, Dijon.

*Opposite*

*Dijon Altarpiece*
Left wing, detail of
*The Annunciation.*

*The Visitation*; on the right, *The Presentation of Christ* and *The Flight into Egypt.*

The first three of these scenes are drawn from the Gospel according to St Luke, and the fourth from that of St Matthew. The artist, however, has made changes in the biblical narrative, and introduced additional symbols, some of which are quite straightforward, others somewhat obscure. This symbolism, and in particular the emblematic use of flowers, has fascinated art historians, who have offered many divergent interpretations of the pictures. The lily with four flowers, which stands between Mary and the angel Gabriel in the foreground of the *Annunciation*, is not problematic, being a well-established symbol of virginity. Behind the angel is a small garden, where roses are trained up an espalier. These too have been seen as a symbol of virginity; but they have also been interpreted as a reference to both the joys of the Virgin, embodied in the blooms, and her pains, represented by the spines. In the garden, moreover, there is a columbine, which has been variously interpreted as an emblem of suffering and death, as well as the symbol of Christ, saviour of the world (the columbine was well-known for its medicinal properties). Even the humble nettle which has somehow strayed into the panel has been put to work by the painter, as a reminder of the omnipresence of vice.

Other commentators have drawn attention to the angel bowing before Mary, with his curly hair and elegant figure, as if he were a heavenly troubador pledging allegiance to his lady. Mary's ultramarine cloak and her brocade dress of blue and gold, with its details picked out in red, are of the style which was favoured at that time by ladies of the Burgundian court. It would seem that even in the cut of his figures' clothes, Broederlam may have been following instructions from his patron, Philip the Bold.

Likewise, the *Visitation* is not a literal rendering of the Bible story. Broederlam gives us the essence of St Luke's text: Mary, already pregnant with the Infant Jesus, meets her cousin Elizabeth who, although supposedly barren, is now by the grace of God expecting a child in her old age. In the painting, the two women are depicted side by side. Mary wears a large blue cloak which she gathers round herself with one hand, while with her free hand she gestures towards Elizabeth. The older woman is dressed in red and green, her head veiled in a fine white material. Although the painter has followed the Scriptures by setting the scene in a mountainous landscape, according to the Gospel the two women meet inside Zacharias's house and not, as here, outdoors, in the shadow of a steep rocky cliff.

The most distinctive aspect of this work is the arrangement of sacred architectural settings which occupy virtually all of two out of the four scenes. At the moment of the Annunciation, Mary is sitting in a small pavilion attached to a much larger and

MELCHIOR BROEDERLAM
*Dijon Altarpiece*
Left wing, detail of
*The Annunciation.*
Musée des Beaux-Arts, Dijon.

*Opposite*
*Dijon Altarpiece*
Detail of right wing,
*The Presentation of Christ.*

much grander building behind. The slender rib vaults, the two windows surmounted by clover-leaf tracery, and the rectangular paving mark the style as gothic. But the relationship between the pavilion and the surrounding space is unusual, as is the way the room is opened out on two sides in order to afford an unimpeded view of the Virgin. The same is true of the temple in *The Presentation of Christ*. The Holy Family, Saint Simeon and a servant girl, who carries a candle in her right hand and a basket with two doves in her left, all gather round the Christ Child. Again, the building in which they stand is open onto the world outside, as if the painter were trying to show us both interior and exterior simultaneously. This apparent contradiction is a convention which Broederlam has borrowed from the paintings of the Italian Trecento, where similar buildings are to be found in the works of Giotto and Ambrosio Lorenzetti, among others.

Yet despite their openness and despite the plants and flowers that hug their bases, these buildings are not part of the landscape but stand apart from nature. This is not entirely Broederlam's fault. The general principles of central perspective were not discovered and codified until fifty years later, in Florence, through the work of Brunelleschi and Alberti respectively. In Broederlam's days, they were known only in a fragmentary form. That is why he uses a hesitant and oblique form of perspective, creating multiple horizons and vanishing points, just like his Italian contemporaries. The Dijon altarpiece even has a gold background. This convention had been used since the Byzantine period and throughout the Middle Ages to symbolize paradise, the realm of the soul, according to the theological conceptions of the time. Broederlam does not respect the convention entirely, for as well as a pair of angels and God the Father, his golden sky also has a bird flying through it. He uses the gold background to link the four scenes together, but achieves this aim at the expense of visual coherence, for such an abstract heaven does not really square with the attempt at perspectival space. The function of perspective is to define a three-dimensional world in which the visible and the real are one. Over the centuries that followed, artists would come to understand and exploit this potential in an increasingly clear manner.

Broederlam's landscape, also, is inspired by the art of the Italian Trecento. In each panel, nature is summarized as a steep rocky outcrop, with a few bushes and flowers clinging to its crevices. As such, it is wholly out of proportion with both the buildings that stand in it and the figures who are moving through it. This is the kind of landscape which is to be found in the school of Siena, and in Giotto's frescos for the Upper Church at Assisi. Since the early 14th century, Flemish artists had been in contact

MELCHIOR BROEDERLAM
*Dijon Altarpiece*
Right wing, detail of
*The Flight into Egypt.*
Musée des Beaux-Arts, Dijon.

*Opposite*
*Dijon Altarpiece*
Detail of left wing,
*The Visitation.*

with their Italian counterparts, some of whose works had reached France. Out of these encounters, an international style had been created, based on the art of Italy, but which was soon equally to be found in Cologne, Prague or Dijon. It is hardly surprising that Broederlam also made use of this artistic lingua franca.

The most significant of the four scenes depicted here is the fourth, representing *The Flight into Egypt*. The Gospel according to St Matthew relates this episode in a few succinct words: "And Joseph rose and took the child and his mother by night, and departed to Egypt." With only this brief indication from the original text, painters have always had to draw on other sources in order to add flesh to their images.

In the Dijon altarpiece, the Virgin is seen in profile, riding side-saddle on a small donkey. She holds the baby Jesus pressed to her cheek. He is wrapped in swaddling bands, and she has drawn her large cloak up around him. The child and his mother are looking at each other. St Joseph is leading the donkey by the halter, while he pours drink into his mouth from a small keg. He carries a stick over his left shoulder, from which his coat and a small pot with a ladle have been hung. He is wearing a hood and a surcoat held in by a leather belt at the waist. He has slipped his purse under the belt, and his leather boots seem to have been worn out by the long journey he has made on foot. He has a hooked nose, a curly beard and bushy eyebrows. The Holy Family have turned out of a sunken road running alongside a stream, and are about to climb a twisting path that leads away to the right across an arid mountainside. In the foreground, the water that wells up out of the rock is collected in a small rectangular basin, from which it pours out through a spout to flow away freely once again. At the foot of the mountain stands a small statue of a warrior, armed with a lance. The statue has been broken in two, an allusion to the end of idolatry. A castle is perched high up on the peak of the mountain, well above the scene.

The heads of the Virgin and Child, unlike that of Joseph, are both surrounded by a golden halo. Indeed, Joseph hardly corresponds to the conventional idea of a saint at all. Broederlam has portrayed him as a rough working man, a tired labourer weighed down by his heavy clothes. Some have even called him a tramp, and suggested that it may not be water with which he is slaking his thirst, but something stronger. Perhaps such stern judgements are themselves merely one reflection of the ambivalent cult that grew up around the figure of Joseph towards the end of the Middle Ages, for it was at that time that he began to be openly caricatured, and depicted as a peasant who deserved to be ridiculed rather than revered. What really distinguished Broederlam's Joseph however is the fact that he is the only ordinary man in the whole altarpiece. He marks the first appearance in painting of an irremediably earthbound reality. From then on, from the Van Eyck brothers to Quentin Massys, this reality would be a constant theme of Flemish artists, even though their work was essentially religious in inspiration. Henceforth, there would be a continuous and growing emphasis on the physicality of the figures depicted, and the details of their appearance, as artists sought to capture their individuality by endowing them with a tangible presence. It is in this sense that Broederlam's Joseph signals the beginning of one of the most significant revolutions in the history of the visual arts.

Broederlam was rediscovered in the early 19th century by the curator of the Dijon Museum, C. Févret de Saint-Mémin, during his researches in the archives of the chartreuse de Champmol. It was Févret de Saint-Mémin who bought the altarpiece for the Dijon Museum. If today we have a sound grasp of the painting's history and its significance, it is largely thanks to the work of two researchers affiliated to France's National Research Centre for Early Flemish Art[1]. Without their efforts, Broederlam and his masterpiece would doubtless still be buried in the obscurity from which they have only recently emerged.

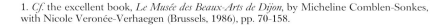

1. *Cf.* the excellent book, *Le Musée des Beaux-Arts de Dijon*, by Micheline Comblen-Sonkes, with Nicole Veronée-Verhaegen (Brussels, 1986), pp. 70-158.

# FOUNDING FATHERS

During the first decades of the 15th century, three great painters laid the foundations of the Flemish school of art. They were Jan Van Eyck, Robert Campin, who was also known as "the Master of Flémalle", and Rogier Van der Weyden. Unlike their Italian contemporaries, they were not theoreticians and their use of perspective was essentially empirical. But they were masters in the techniques of oil painting, an art in which Jan Van Eyck would long remain unsurpassed. It was this that gave their work such extraordinary sophistication in the handling of detail.

In devoting themselves to the faithful copying of everyday life, their motive was always a spiritual one. For them, naturalism was itself a religious attitude, for they believed God to be present in every element of His creation. It was Jan Van Eyck who was to carry this passion for detail to its limits, even to the detriment of subjectivity and emotion, in both his major sacred compositions and his portraits. Rogier Van der Weyden, on the other hand, sought above all to create religious art that would enrich the viewer's emotional experience of their shared faith.

Their contemporary Petrus Christus has too often been dismissed as a mere disciple of Van Eyck and Van der Weyden. Yet he was an innovator too, for he was the first Flemish artist to master the new technique for the visual representation of reality – the principles of linear perspective.

ROGIER VAN DER WEYDEN
*The Last Judgement*
Detail.
Hôtel-Dieu, Beaune.

# HUBERT AND JAN VAN EYCK

In the past, art historians, for various reasons, have sometimes cast doubt on the existence of Hubert Van Eyck. Today, however, no one still seriously claims that the elder brother of Jan, Lambert and Margareta Van Eyck never existed. He was born at Maeseyck, near Mons, though the date of his birth is unknown. The name Hubert itself, which was not common in Ghent, may well indicate his foreign origin. A few facts can be gleaned from his tombstone, which is now in the Lapidary Museum in St Bavo's Abbey. An inscription engraved on a copper plate which has since disappeared but which was once affixed to the stone, recorded 18 September 1426 as the date of his death. However, the most crucial piece of information to have come down to us is the quatrain inscribed on the frame of the *Adoration of the Lamb*, the Van Eyck brothers' most celebrated work. The verse was placed there when the altarpiece was installed on 6 May 1432. It states that the polyptych was begun by Pictor Hubertus Eyck, and finished by his brother Jan, at the request of Jodocus Vijd, deputy burgomaster of Ghent, warden of the church of St John, and of his wife, Elisabeth Borluut, who commissioned it. The quatrain was discovered in 1823. Although its authenticity was once contested it is now generally recognized as genuine.

An additional argument for the existence of Hubert is provided by a stylistic analysis of the painting, in which the work of two different hands can be clearly discerned. The overall conception of the altarpiece is certainly the work of Hubert, along with the execution of certain parts, such as the panels in the lower tier. Here, the manner is archaic, and reflects the continuing dominance of the international style that was practised by Broederlam. The composition is typically unoriginal: the landscape is still conceived as a distant background, with which the figures at the

*Above*

HUBERT AND JAN VAN EYCK
*Polyptych The Adoration
of the Lamb*
Detail of left wing,
*Angels Singing.*
St Bavo's Cathedral, Ghent.

*Opposite*
*Polyptych The Adoration
of the Lamb*
Detail of right wing,
*Angels with Instruments.*

HUBERT AND JAN VAN EYCK
*Polyptych The Adoration of the Lamb*
Detail of left wing closed.
St Bavo's Cathedral, Ghent.

front have no organic relation, an effect that is reinforced by the bird's eye point of view.

According to tradition, Jan Van Eyck was also born at Maeseyck; but we can only vaguely conjecture the date of his birth on the basis of much later biographical information. Nor do we know anything of his artistic training. What we do know is that he entered the service of John of Bavaria, Count of Holland and of Zeeland, and Prince-Bishop elect of Liège, as a painter and honorary equerry. With his many assistants, he worked at the Binnenhof in The Hague. After his protector's death, he entered the service of Philip the Good on 19 May 1425. He settled in Lille – which, together with Brussels and Ghent, was part of the central administrative structure of the Duchy of Flanders and Burgundy – some time before 2 August 1425. On 26 August 1426, the painter – who was already well-known for his spirit of adventure – was paid to undertake a lengthy pilgrimage-cum-secret mission for the Duke. On 27 October of the same year he received money from the same source again, this time for "certain distant and secret journeys".

Some of these payments may also have related to an embassy the painter undertook to Valencia in Spain in 1426. His task on that occasion was to ask Alfonso V of Aragon for the hand of his niece Isabella of Urgel on behalf of Philip the Good. Jan Van Eyck's presence in Aragon would seem to be proved by the interest Alfonso subsequently took in his painting. The Spanish King bought several works from him and, between 1431 and 1436, sent his official painter, Luis Dalmau, to Flanders to study with Van Eyck. He wanted Dalmau to learn the secrets of oil painting, which at that time the artists of Burgundy tended to think of as their exclusive privilege. When negotiations in Valencia came to nought, Philip the Good then sent an embassy to Portugal to request the hand of the infanta Isabella in marriage. A contemporary report confirms that the painter Jan Van Eyck took part in this mission as well. Van Eyck painted two portraits of the Portuguese princess at the castle of Aviz in January 1429. Messengers then conveyed these portraits to Philip the Good. Travelling by sea and by land, they managed to reach Flanders by 1 February. Van Eyck's journeys must have contributed in no small way to the growing interest in Flemish painting that was evinced by the courts, nobility and bourgeoisie of Portugal and Spain.

He also undertook a highly confidential mission beyond the confines of Christian Europe, as part of Philip the Good's plans for a crusade. We will probably never know anything for certain of the content of Jan Van Eyck's "secret missions". But it seems possible that he was sent to reconnoitre Muslim roads and territories in southern Spain and perhaps even further afield. He would then have been expected to produce maps that could later be used for military intelligence. All we know for sure is that he was valued by the States of Burgundy not only as an exceptional painter, but also as a distinguished diplomat, and even, on occasions, as a skilled spy.

After many adventures, both artistic and diplomatic, Jan Van Eyck at last tired of his foreign missions. In 1432 he bought a house in Bruges and, at about the same time, he married a certain Margareta. The time had now come to live and paint in peace. A first child was born to the couple in 1434. The Duke of Burgundy did not forget this most loyal of artists and over the years sent Van Eyck many presents on the occasion of each successive addition to the family. An account survives for the expenses of Van Eyck's funeral, which was held in the church of St Donatian in Bruges. Since the church was closed for worship as of 23 June 1441, it seems likely Van Eyck died shortly before this date. He was regarded as a member of the Duke's family, and was thus entitled to the exceptional privilege of burial in the cloister beside the church. The following year, his brother Lambert arranged for his tomb to be moved inside the church. Although we do not know the date of his birth, his biographers have always supposed than Jan Van Eyck died young.

Almost nothing has survived of the commissions he carried out for Philip the Good. We know that he worked on the decoration of the Duke's residences at Hesdin (1431 or 1432), Brussels (1433) and Lille (1434). We also know that he painted portraits of Philip the Good and of his family, which have unfortunately been lost. Of his surviving works, only one is generally agreed to have been a commission for the Duke: an *Annunciation* painted for the chartreuse de Champmol. Yet although he was an official painter to the court, Jan Van Eyck was always free to work for other clients. It was in this way that he came to paint the *Adoration of the Lamb* which, according to the dedication inscribed on it, was consecrated on 3 May 1432.

This polyptych is mystical, not to say esoteric, in intention, and is imbued throughout with both spiritual and intellectual signification. When opened, it represents the communion of saints, which is "the new heaven and the new earth", in the words of the Revelation of St John. Thus the central panel of the lower tier portrays the saints symbolizing the eight Beatitudes gathered round the altar where the sacrifice of the Lamb is taking place, at the centre of the heavenly garden which has sprung from His blood.

To left and right, in the foreground, are two processions facing one another. One of these is made up of the Old Testament patriarchs and prophets, and the other of figures from the New

HUBERT AND JAN VAN EYCK
*Polyptych The Adoration of the Lamb*
Detail of right wing closed.
St Bavo's Cathedral, Ghent.

*This page*

HUBERT AND JAN VAN EYCK

*Polyptych The Adoration of the Lamb*
(closed)

*Opposite*

*Polyptych The Adoration of the Lamb*
1427-1432, oil on wood,
375×320 cm (148×126 in).
St Bavo's Cathedral, Ghent.

Testament. Some of them are kneeling, barefoot. Behind them is assembled the hierarchy of the Church – popes, deacons and bishops, wearing sumptuous jewelry and clothes in the bright red of martyrdom. In the background are two further groups, facing each other as if they had just emerged from the surrounding shrubbery. These are, on one side, the Confessors of the Faith, tightly packed together and almost all dressed in blue; and on the other side, the Virgin Martyrs, holding out palm fronds and wearing in their hair crowns of flowers of a kind traditionally worn by young girls at certain holy ceremonies. In the middle of the panel, around the altar where the Lamb spills forth his blood, angels kneel, holding the emblems of His Passion. Grace is symbolized by a radiant dove hovering in the sky, and eternal life is represented by a fountain in the foreground. A paradisiacal landscape runs across all five lower panels, uniting them in a single

composition. It is strewn with plants from different countries and flowers of different seasons. The central panel is vibrant with green, while those to the sides are more arid and rocky. The horizon sits high in the frame and is closed off by groves of trees, behind which clusters of fairy-tale buildings can be made out, representing the heavenly Jerusalem.

The community of saints also extends onto the side panels. Magnificently arrayed horsemen, representing the Soldiers of Christ, are followed by the Just Judges. Opposite them are the Holy Hermits who have renounced the world, and the Pilgrim Saints, who were favourite figures of identification throughout the Middle Ages. They are led by a giant of a man, St Christopher. Many later commentators have suggested that his great height would have reminded the contemporary viewer of Jodocus Vijd's brother, also called Christopher. In the middle of the upper tier

is God Almighty, the Word, essence and origin of the universe. He is dressed in red and is crowned with a magnificent tiara. On his left is Mary and on his right, St John the Baptist. These central figures are surrounded by angels who are singing or playing instruments. At the far right and left of the composition respectively are the figures of Adam and Eve. They were painted by Jan Van Eyck, and are set into trompe-l'œil niches. Light and shadow play delicately over their forms which stand out as though they had been sculpted in the round.

The realism of these two figures struck contemporary viewers forcefully, and this style continues on the outside of the panels when the altarpiece is closed. The external decoration shows sibyls and prophets, the kneeling figures of the donors, and the Annunciation with the angel Gabriel and the Virgin Mary.

We must be careful not to exaggerate the significance of this realism. It in no way represents "progress", whether technical or aesthetic, in the means of representation. Its increasing use should rather be attributed to a change in the theological motives

*Above*

HUBERT AND JAN VAN EYCK
*Polyptych The Adoration of the Lamb*
Detail of left wing closed,
*The Annunciation.*
St Bavo's Cathedral, Ghent.

*Below right*

*Polyptych The Adoration of the Lamb*
Detail of central panel, *The Virgin Martyrs.*

*Opposite*

*Polyptych The Adoration of the Lamb*
Detail of right wing closed,
*The Annunciation.*

of the age. During the Middle Ages, official doctrine had placed earthly realities on the lowest level of the scale of Creation – if they were not, indeed, the work of the devil himself. However, by the time of the Van Eyck brothers, religious thought had begun to absorb the influence of the great mystics. People began to view the entire world as the work of God, the source of all creation, and present in its every detail, no matter how small and insignificant. Thus nature came to be seen as sacred, as it was a reflection of God's spirit. Where mediaeval art had focussed on a world beyond this world, the new art was devoted to scrupulous observation of what lay before the artist's eyes. Imagination was replaced by attention. Every creature, every thing, was now perceived as a sign – a metaphor – representing a spiritual truth. This vision determined the artist's vocation: to imitate the visible world as faithfully as possible, not merely in order to glorify creation, but so as to reveal the metaphysical dimension that lay concealed within.

*The Adoration of the Lamb* is a first, partial realisation of this new approach which was to run through all of Jan Van Eyck's

work. Its importance to him can be judge if we turn to the *Madonna with Chancellor Rolin* in the Louvre.

Nicolas Rolin, who commissioned this work, was a man with a forceful personality. Despite his humble background, he was highly intelligent and eventually rose to hold the highest offices of State. For over forty years he was Philip the Good's right-hand man, and one of the principal architects of the monarch's success. Van Eyck painted him when he was already in his sixties. His face, though marked by the heavy responsibilities he has had to bear, still fascinates the viewer with the sense of energy and will-power which it projects. Rolin is wearing a gold brocade jacket trimmed with mink. He kneels at prayer on the left of the composition. His gaze is pensive, looking as though he has just raised his eyes from his book of hours. On the right is the seated figure of the Virgin. Wrapped in a voluminous red robe, she is presenting the Infant Jesus to the chancellor while a hovering angel holds a magnificent crown above her head. The figures have been brought together in the loggia of an Italianate palace. The three arches through which the space opens out behind them seem rather large in relation to their immediate surroundings. They give first onto a small garden with lilies and roses symbolizing Mary's virtues. Slightly farther back are two small figures, one standing at an oblique angle to the viewer and the other with his back to us. Near them are two peacocks, symbols of immortality, but perhaps also of the pride to which such a powerful man as Chancellor Rolin might well succumb.

The most surprising feature in this splendid picture is without doubt the townscape that stretches out beyond the loggia. The crenellated battlements indicate that the palace is in fact a fortress, built on the edge of an escarpment. Below, a broad

JAN VAN EYCK
*Madonna with
Chancellor Rolin*
Detail.
Musée du Louvre,
Paris.

JAN VAN EYCK
*The Arnolfini Marriage*
1434, oil on wood,
81.8 × 59.7 cm (32 × 23 1/2 in).
National Gallery, London.

*Opposite*

*The Arnolfini Marriage*
Detail.

meandering river with an island in its midst flows through the heart of a city. The two banks of the river are linked by a fortified bridge. The humbler areas of the town lie to the left, behind Chancellor Rolin. On the right, behind the Virgin, are the wealthy quarters, with a profusion of buildings, dominated by an imposing gothic church. Countless tiny figures are flocking towards this part of town, across the bridge and through the roads and squares. Meanwhile on the river, boats are arriving and putting into shore. It is as if all mankind, united by faith, were travelling in pilgrimage towards this city and its cathedral. In the distance, the horizon is closed off by snow-capped mountains under a pinky-yellow sky. In the opinion of Charles de Tolnay, this painting represents a comprehensive vision of the entire universe.

Van Eyck's painting of the *Arnolfini Marriage* is mainly famous for the circular mirror that hangs on the wall behind the couple. Giovanni Arnolfini, a prosperous Italian banker who had settled in Bruges, and his wife Giovanna Cenami, stand side by side in the bridal chamber, facing towards the viewer. The husband is holding out his wife's hand. Despite the restricted space, the painter has contrived to surround them with a host of symbols. To the left, the oranges placed on the low table and the window-sill are a reminder of an original innocence, of an age before sin. Unless, that is, they are not in fact oranges but apples (it is difficult to be certain), in which case they would represent the temptation of knowledge and the Fall. Above the couple's heads, the candle that has been left burning in broad daylight on one of the branches of an ornate copper chandelier can be interpreted as the nuptial flame, or as the eye of God. The small dog in the foreground is an emblem of fidelity and love. Meanwhile, the marriage bed with its bright red curtains evokes the physical act of love which, according to Christian doctrine, is an essential part of the perfect union of man and wife. Although all these different elements are highly charged with meaning, they are of secondary importance compared to the mirror, the focal point of the whole composition. It has often been noted that two tiny figures can be seen reflected in it, their image captured as they cross the threshold of the room. They are the painter himself and a young man, doubtless arriving to act as witnesses to the marriage. The essential point, however, is the fact that the convex mirror is able to absorb and reflect in a single image both the floor and the ceiling of the room, as well as the sky and the garden outside, both of which are otherwise barely visible through the side window. The mirror thus acts as a sort of hole in the texture of space. It sucks the entire visual world into itself, transforming it into a representation. The cubic space in which the Arnolfinis stand is itself a prefiguration of the techniques of perspective which were still to come. Van Eyck practised perspective on a purely heuristic

JAN VAN EYCK
*Madonna with Canon van der Paele*
1436, oil on wood, 122 × 157 cm (48 × 62 in).
Groeninge Museum, Bruges.

basis, unaware of the laws by which it was governed. In this picture, he uses the mirror precisely in order to explode the limits of the space to which his technique gives him access as soon as it threatens to limit him.

Vasari claimed that it was Van Eyck who had invented oil painting. We know now that he was wrong, for in fact this technique would seem to date back to Antiquity – if we are to believe Pliny the Elder. Yet it is true that Van Eyck pioneered the use of new binders, thanks to which it was possible to make wet-on-dry alterations, and thus obtain nuances and forms of transparency that were previously unimaginable. These techniques help to explain his extraordinary ability to render the psychology of his sitters. As we have seen, his Chancellor Rolin is energetic and self-willed. His Arnolfini, on the other hand, with his sly and menacing face, lives up to his reputation as a man without moral scruples (his nickname was Cunning Hernoud). The bald wrinkled head of the old canon in the *Madonna with Canon Van der Paele* is an equally impressive exercise in psychological analysis. Van Eyck was a great portraitist, only equalled by Rogier Van der Weyden. He rejected the portrait in profile, which allowed the character of the sitter to be reduced to a simple silhouette, preferring instead to paint his subjects full or three-quarter face, which allowed him to introduce many subtle details and nuances. The gruff, peremptory *Portrait of Baudouin de Lannoy*, knight of the Golden Fleece, that of the painter's own wife *Margareta*, pictured gazing at her husband with clear calm eyes, and that of the substantial figure of *Cardinal Niccolo Albergati* are all three masterpieces.

Each of the twenty or so paintings by Van Eyck that have survived creates its own luminous jewel-like fragment of space. Every object is haloed with light, which emphasizes form and volume and reveals, through its reflections and refractions, the quality and texture of the material from which the object is made. The painter's attention to minute details which, though scarcely visible, are meticulously copied as if by means of a magnifying glass, reinforces the suggestive power of his work. Facius, a contemporary chronicler, described Jan Van Eyck as a learned man, intellectually curious, with a good command of Latin, and a more than rudimentary knowledge of Hebrew and Greek. He was able to transpose the most subtle theological concepts into tangible images, and was completely at home in the complex world of symbols. In any event, his work today stands witness to his astonishing knowledge of anatomy, geography (among his works is a *mappa mundi*), geology, botany, chemistry and all the achievements of human industry: architecture, sculpture, cartography, navigation, jewelry, embroidery, cabinetwork, metallurgy and the martial arts. Along with his brother Hubert, Jan Van Eyck must be counted as one of the greatest artists of this golden age of Flemish painting.

JAN VAN EYCK
*Portrait of Cardinal Niccolo Albergati*
C. 1435-1438, oil on wood,
35 × 29 cm (14 × 11 1/2 in).
Kunsthistorisches Museum, Vienna.

*Following page, left*
JAN VAN EYCK
*Portrait of Margareta van Eyck*
1439, oil on wood, 32.6 × 25.8 cm (13 × 10 in).
Groeninge Museum, Bruges.

*Following page, right*
JAN VAN EYCK
*Portrait of Baudouin de Lannoy*
1437, oil on wood, 26 × 19.5 cm (10 × 7 1/2 in).
Staatliche Museen, Berlin.

# ROBERT CAMPIN
## THE MASTER OF FLÉMALLE

The master of Flémalle, perhaps the most popular of all Flemish painters, never existed. He was the invention of a German historian, Hugo von Tschudi, who in 1908 brought together under this name several works that had originally been attributed to Rogier Van der Weyden, but which were clearly not by the latter painter. At that time, the pictures were believed to have come from the abbey of Flémalle, near Liège. This supposition, however, was false, and in fact we now know that no such abbey of Flémalle ever existed. Although there is no reliable information as to the place of origin of these works, their attribution is fortunately a less mysterious matter. The historian Hulin de Loo first pointed out that the pictures present a stylistic affinity with those of Rogier, albeit in a somewhat more archaic vein, and accordingly concluded that they were the work of Van der Weyden's master, Robert Campin.

We know the approximate date of Campin's birth (between 1375 and 1379) but not the place. We do know, however, that in 1410 he paid dues as a burgher of Tournai, and it was there that he married Ysabiel Stoquain, seven years his elder. The couple had no children and Campin died in Tournai in 1444. This was an unsettled period in Flanders, and Campin's life was far from uneventful, as is revealed by the laconic and impersonal references to the painter to be found in the municipal archives. In 1423, Tournai was the scene of a popular uprising. The aristocratic authorities were overthrown and replaced by a democratic government, in which Campin himself played a leading role. The new government survived until 1428. During this brief interval, Campin held several different offices: first as dean of the Guild of St Luke (the painters' and metalworkers' guild) and then, beginning in 1428, as warden of the church of St Peter. The following year he was found guilty of having participated in the uprising and was sentenced to pay a fine and make a pilgrimage

*Above and opposite*
ROBERT CAMPIN
**The Nativity**
Details.
Musée des Beaux-Arts, Dijon.

*Opposite*

ROBERT CAMPIN
*The Nativity*
1420, oil on wood,
87 × 70 cm (34 1/2 × 27 1/2 in).
Musée des Beaux-Arts, Dijon.

*Following pages, left*

ROBERT CAMPIN
*The Crucified Thief*
C. 1410, oil on wood,
33 × 92.5 cm (13 × 36 1/2 in).
Städelsches Kunstinstitut, Frankfurt.

*Following pages, right*

ROBERT CAMPIN
*The Holy Trinity*
C. 1410, oil on wood,
148.7 × 61 cm (58 1/2 × 24 in).
Städelsches Kunstinstitut, Frankfurt.

to Saint Gilles in Provence. He was also forbidden henceforth to hold public office in the town. In 1432, he once again found himself in court, this time accused of adultery. It was claimed that, while still married, he was leading a "lewd and dissolute life" with a certain Laurence Polette. He was banished from Tournai for one year, but thanks to the intervention of Margaret of Burgundy, his sentence was commuted to a fine.

Falling foul of the law in this way seriously damaged both his career and his posthumous reputation, even though churches and individuals continued to give him commissions. It is doubtless on this account that after his death his work was almost entirely neglected until very recently. The first written sources for the history of Flemish art, on which Vasari and many others based their accounts and on which modern historians still largely depend, are the work of foreign courtiers who visited Flanders. Convention dictated that the outstanding figure of the day was Jan Van Eyck, the very model of a court painter. As for Robert Campin, he was far from living up to these chroniclers' conception of respectability. He had doubly discredited himself in the eyes of the aristocracy and the bourgeoisie: first by his behaviour during the Tournai uprising, and then again by courting scandal in his personal life.

His most famous work is the *Nativity*, painted in 1420, which hangs today in the musée des Beaux-Arts at Dijon. It is unusual in that it juxtaposes on a single panel three distinct episodes from the life of Christ: the Nativity proper, the legend of the midwives, and the adoration of the shepherds. The child and his parents are shown on the threshold of a rather ramshackle wooden stable. The thatched roof has a hole in it and the walls are dilapidated, revealing the ox and the ass, who, untypically for such a composition, have turned their backs on the newborn infant, rather than drawing near to warm him with their breath. The Virgin is kneeling, her hands held out in a gesture of adoration and her eyes lowered. At her feet, the Christ Child lies on the bare earth, radiant with light. Joseph, who had been a figure of mockery throughout the Middle Ages and even as recently as Broederlam, is here presented as a venerable old man. He holds a candle in one hand, and with the other shelters its flame from the wind. In the foreground, on the right of the composition, are the two midwives who, according to an apocryphal Gospel, were summoned by Joseph in a moment of anxiety. Behind this first group, the upper part of a stable door has swung wide open to reveal the three shepherds, seemingly prevented from approaching any closer by awe and respect.

Hovering above the scene are four angels. As if exempted from the laws of gravity, they sweep past borne on the wind.

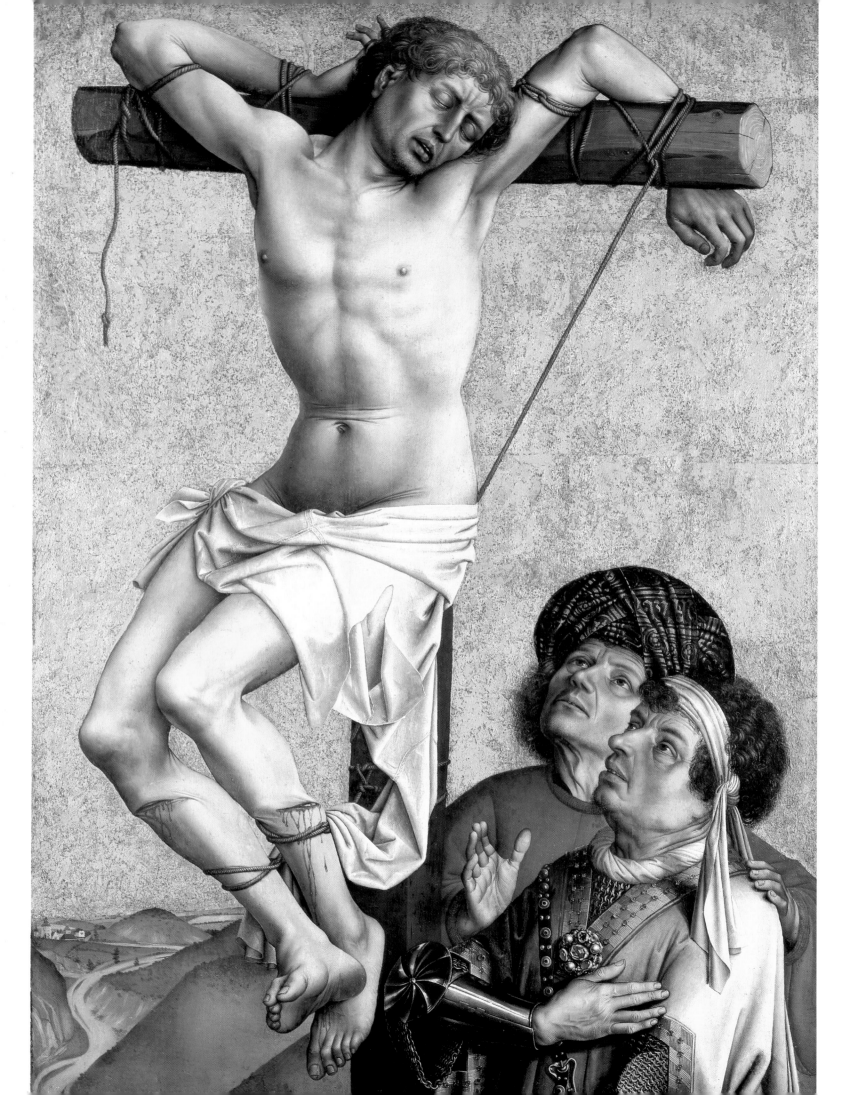

They are holding phylacteries, on one of which is written a message. It is addressed to one of the midwives, whose right hand is paralysed: *"Tangue puerum et sanabaris"* ("touch the child and you shall be healed"). As in the art of the Van Eyck brothers, Campin's painting is minutely detailed in its realism. Light is an important stylistic and symbolic element: the candle which St Joseph holds alight even though it is day reminds the viewer that Jesus was born during the night, and that darkness gave way suddenly to light, as the laws of nature were overturned. And how can one avoid thinking, in this context, of another analogous phenomenon – the darkness at noon that marked the moment of the Saviour's death?

The most striking element in this Nativity, however, is certainly the extended landscape that spreads out behind the stable. Beyond the two midwives, a rutted track running beside a stream leads the eye deep into the picture space. The track is bordered by pollarded willows and tall trees with fine branches. A path joins the track and leads across a meadow surrounded by a wicker fence. A man and a woman are walking along the path; they are wearing capes and are accompanied by a peasant woman carrying a basket of eggs on her head. Further on is a large farmhouse, its yard surrounded by high walls, and beyond this again lies a village with its houses, a lake nestling between hills and a small farm with vineyards perched on a slope. To the left of these stands a town with many splendid buildings, above which a small castle sits perched on a rocky outcrop. It is winter, but the sun is still visible between two mountain peaks, its rays spreading out from the golden disk in a symbol of renewal and redemption.

In his *Nativity*, Campin proved himself a sensitive painter of landscape, who knew how to portray the atmospheric subtleties of light and air; but he does not always use nature as the background for his compositions. In *The Crucified Thief*, the one surviving panel from a lost altarpiece, now in Frankfurt, he resorts to the archaic device of a gold background, contrasting its abstraction with the marked individuality of the figures. The thief's face is contorted with pain, and the wounds where the cords have cut into the flesh are rendered in an extraordinarily brutal manner. The Roman soldiers looking on, particularly the one whose curly hair is held back by a white band and who is placing one hand on his heart, are portrayed with a realism that was at that time outstanding. In other monumental figure paintings, such as the Frankfurt *Virgin and Child* and *St Veronica*, Campin uses a background of brocade hangings to produce a space without depth. These two pictures contrast strongly with the third panel of the triptych, a grisaille *Holy Trinity* which is treated in an illusionistic manner as a statue sculpted in the round.

The same brute force visible in the Frankfurt paintings was already evident in the *Seilern Triptych*, named after its present owner, the Count of Seilern. It was painted between 1410 and 1420, and is considered to be the earliest of Campin's works to have survived to the present day. There is an excellent analysis of this painting by Jellie Dijkstra[1]. The central panel represents the entombment: the Virgin, Joseph of Arimathea, Nicodemus and another Mary are holding Christ's body spread out on its shroud above the tomb. The other figures in the scene function as so many allusions to different stages in the Passion cycle: St John, on whom the Virgin leans, refers us to the Lamentation; Mary Magdalen rubbing oil into Christ's feet is a reminder of his Anointment; the woman who is holding up a piece of material is probably St Veronica, and her presence alludes to Calvary; finally, the angels who are carrying the instruments of the Passion represent the Crucifixion. The left wing depicts a donor. Behind the figure stands the hill of Golgotha. The central cross between the two thieves has been left empty, with a ladder propped against it, to remind us of the Descent from the Cross. The right wing represents the Resurrection. The gold background of all three panels

*Above*
ROBERT CAMPIN
*Seilern Triptych*
1410-1420, oil on wood.
Courtauld Institute, London.

*Opposite, left*
ROBERT CAMPIN
*Virgin and Child*
C. 1410, oil on wood, 160 × 68 cm
(63 × 27 in).
Städelsches Kunstistitut, Frankfurt.

*Opposite, right*
ROBERT CAMPIN
*St Veronica*
C. 1410, oil on wood, 151.5 × 61 cm
(59 1/2 × 24 in).
Städelsches Kunstinstitut, Frankfurt.

1. *Cf.* collectif *Les Primitifs flamands et leur temps*, Louvain-La-Neuve, 1994, pp. 323-324.

# ROBERT CAMPIN

ROBERT CAMPIN
*Seilern Triptych*
Central panel, detail of
*The Entombment.*
Courtauld Institute, London.

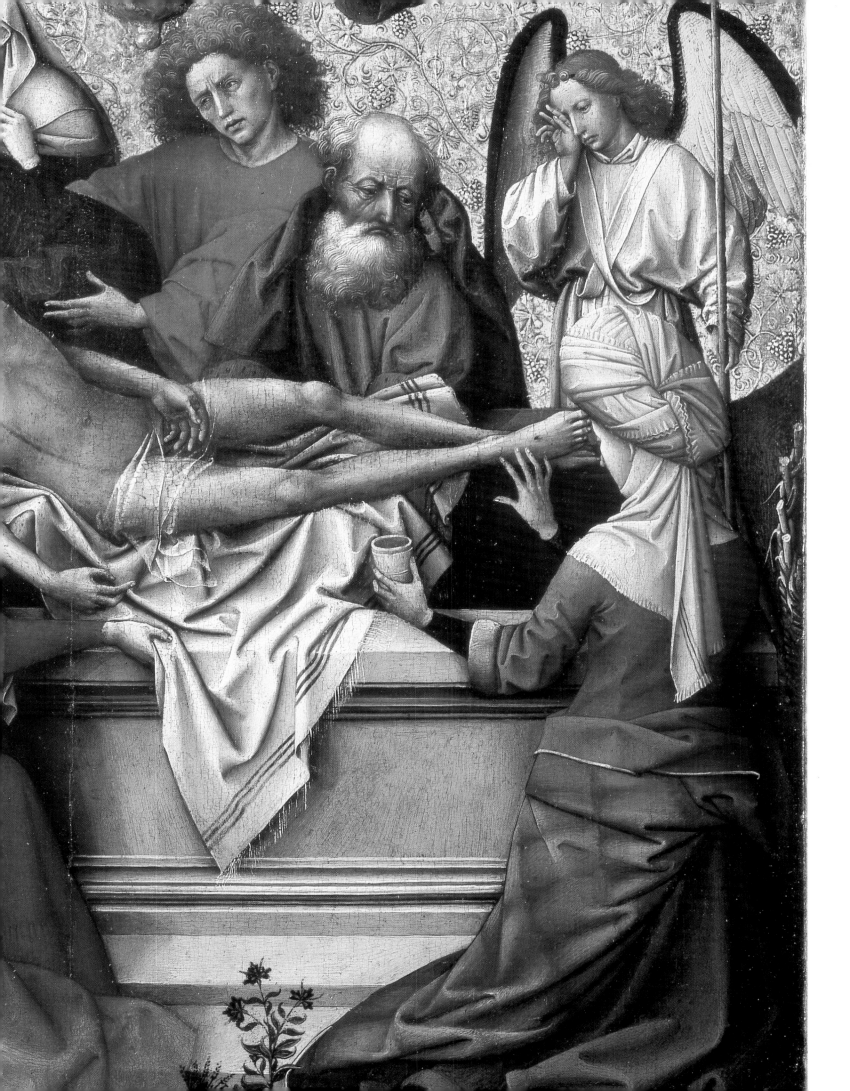

*Heinrich von Werl Triptych*
of which only two panels survive.
C. 1438, oil on wood,
101 × 47 cm (40 × 18 1/2 in).
Museo del Prado, Madrid.

*Opposite, right*

Right wing, *St Barbara.*

*Opposite, left*

Left wing,
*The Donor*
*and St John the Baptist.*

is decorated with a motif of vine branches and grapes, symbols of Christ, the true vine.

The figures in the central panel are noticeably larger than those on the wings. The viewer thus feels closer to the central scene than to those on either side. Otherwise, however, the treatment of space is entirely traditional. On the left wing, for instance, the landscape behind the donor is quite shallow, and the figures are not shown one behind the other, their size reducing according to the laws of perspective, but are ranged vertically and all depicted on the same scale.

If we turn now to a later triptych, painted in 1438 for Heinrich von Werl, we can gauge the extent to which Campin's style has altered. It is because of this change that it has been difficult to identify his various and varied works as the achievement of a single master. Only two panels of the Werl triptych have survived. One depicts *The Donor and St John the Baptist,* and the other *St Barbara,* who is surrounded by many of the symbols traditionally associated with the Virgin (though with certain variations – the lily, for instance, is replaced by an iris). The details are treated in the manner of Jan Van Eyck and there is even a convex circular mirror in the left wing, which reflects the view through the window as well as the two main figures, just as in the *Arnolfini Marriage.* There are also resemblances to Rogier Van der Weyden's *Annunciation* in the Louvre. For instance, Campin and Van der Weyden use the same objects – a transparent sunlit carafe and a curiously shaped dented metal ewer. But the repetition of these objects does not in itself prove that the two pictures are the work of the same painter. Rogier's painting also reproduces a detail from the *Arnolfini Marriage,* the carved chandelier, yet no one has ever suggested that he and Van Eyck might be one and the same artist. But when seen side by side, these three works do demonstrate how closely related was the work of these three great Flemish masters.

There is one final smaller work worthy of mention here: the *Mérode Altarpiece,* to which Charles de Tolnay once devoted a masterly essay. Recently, doubts have arisen as to whether this triptych really is by Robert Campin. Its subject is the Annunciation. Unusually for this theme, however, the right wing depicts Joseph at work in his carpenter's shop. As de Tolnay points out, the Catholic Church has traditionally held that Joseph had six children by a previous marriage, and since at the time he was only Mary's fiancé, not her husband, the couple did not live together. This peculiar assemblage of subjects is therefore extremely rare, not to say unique, in the history of painting. The objects in Joseph's workshop are chosen so as to symbolically prefigure the Passion: the sword-shaped saw in the foreground alludes to the

ıno millemo e qter xto ec ocio lucfeuc elate r uıqu nulíez huıeus Welıs ıngr coloı

*Above*

ROBERT CAMPIN
**Mérode Altarpiece**
1427-1428, oil on wood,
64.1 × 117.8 cm (25 × 46 1/2 in).
Metropolitan Museum of Art, New York.

*Opposite*

**Mérode Altarpiece**
Central panel,
detail of **The Annunciation**

weapon that St Peter would use to cut off Malchus' ear while Christ was being arrested; the log that lies nearby recalls the wood of the cross; the stick propped against it, of the crown of thorns; nails, hammers, pliers and screwdrivers all prefigure the instruments of the Passion. The mousetrap which Joseph is making may be a reference either to Christ's arrest (the mouse being associated, in popular tradition, with the soul) or to the Augustinian doctrine that the Virgin's marriage and Christ's Incarnation were planned by Providence as a trap in which to catch the devil, like a mouse lured by a bait.

It is also possible, however, that this painting is not, in fact, an *Annunciation*. In the left wing, it is clear from the landscape visible behind the donor that it is springtime. The snow flakes falling in the small square that can be glimpsed through the window behind Joseph, on the other hand, suggest that it is winter. If both are true, then the triptych may well be intended to symbolize the time that passed between 25 March and 25 December, between Christ's conception and his birth. In which case, it would best be described as a *Nativity*.

# ROGIER VAN DER WEYDEN

Of all Flemish painters of that period, it was Rogier Van der Weyden who exercised the greatest influence upon contemporary art. He was born in 1399 or 1400, in Tournai, where his father was a master cutler. We know nothing of his youth, save that he married Elisabeth Goffaert, the daughter of a Brussels cobbler, probably in 1426. The couple had four children. Some historians have conjectured that he then went to work in Bruges, others have suggested Louvain. However, we do know that he finally settled in Brussels, thanks to a certificate dated 2 May 1436, on which day he assumed the office of "city painter". Shortly afterwards, Rogier executed four "justice scenes" for the Town Hall, pictures which were intended to encourage judges to deliberate in a spirit of prudence and equity. By this time he was already prosperous. His studio in the Cantersteen, the goldsmiths' quarter of Brussels, expanded steadily throughout his lifetime. By the end of his life, it had become a flourishing, internationally reputed business, where many foreign painters came to learn their craft. In the Jubilee Year of 1450, Rogier made a rare journey to Rome. There he encountered for the first time the work of the Italian masters, although the impact of this discovery on his own work seems to have been limited. He was already a celebrated figure in his own lifetime: in 1453, the German cardinal and philosopher Nicolas of Cusa referred to him in a letter as *"maximus pictor"*.

"Maistre" Rogier Van der Weyden was rich, famous, and successful, but also extremely generous. Many documents have survived to bear witness to this fact. In April 1441, he appeared before the magistrate of Brussels in his capacity as trustee and guardian of an orphaned niece. In 1448, he made a donation of money and paintings to two chartreuses, one at Hérines, near

*Above*

ROGIER VAN DER WEYDEN
*St Luke Drawing a Portrait of the Virgin*
Detail.

*Opposite*

*St Luke Drawing a Portrait of the Virgin*
C. 1450, oil on wood,
138 × 110 cm (54 1/2 × 43 1/2 in).
Alte Pinakothek, Munich.

*Below*

ROGIER VAN DER WEYDEN
**Descent from the Cross**
Before 1443, oil on wood,
220 × 262 cm (86 1/2 × 103 in).
Museo del Prado, Madrid

*Opposite*

**Descent from the Cross**
Detail, **Mary.**

*Following pages, left*

**Descent from the Cross**
Detail, **Magdalen.**

*Following pages, right*

**Descent from the Cross**
Detail, **Jesus Christ.**

Enghien, which his eldest son had recently entered, and the other at Scheut, near Brussels. Between 1455 and 1457, he was a trustee of the infirmary and charitable institution Ter Kisten. His charitable inclination is also revealed in his will, which stipulates that at least two gifts be made to the poor of different parishes in Brussels. From 1462 onwards, he and his wife belonged to the Rosicrucian Brotherhood, whose members represented the elite of Brussels society : aristocrats, courtiers, artists and high-ranking burghers. He died at the height of his fame and powers on 16 or 18 June 1464, followed shortly afterwards by his wife. They are buried together in the collegiate church of St Gudula in Brussels, in front of the altar of St Catherine's chapel, "beneath a blue slab on which there is engraved the figure of a dead man".

Although he was an official painter of his adoptive home town, Rogier Van der Weyden also received many other commissions, both from Flanders and abroad. Stylistic analysis and other scientific and historical methods have enabled us to attribute some forty or so surviving paintings to Rogier – diptychs, triptychs, polyptychs and portraits. Their precise dates are not

always documented, but a rough chronology can be reconstructed thanks to two works the dates of which are attested by independent documentary evidence: the great polyptych of the *Last Judgement* in Beaune, painted between 1442 and 1451, and the *Braque Triptych* in the Louvre, painted between 1450 and 1452, when the painter was at the height of his powers.

Among Van der Weyden's earliest works are two paintings which already demonstrate his genius, though in very different ways. The *Descent from the Cross*, having hung for many years in Notre-Dame-du-Dehors in Louvain, was bought for the Escurial Palace and is today in the Prado collections. It is probably the central panel of a triptych, the wings of which have been lost. The composition represents ten virtually life-size figures in a niche-like space set against a gold background. In the upper part of the picture, the cross has largely been concealed, so as to focus the eye on Christ's body. His rigid corpse lies diagonally across the panel, defining an arabesque form that extends to include the figure of the pale-faced Virgin swooning with grief. Beside them stand John, Nicodemus, Joseph of Arimathea and the holy women. On the far right, the Magdalen wrings her hands in grief. Together, and each in their own way, these figures weave subtle variations on Mary's suffering. This physical expressivity is emphasized by the formal play and counterplay of curved lines. The colours are bright, the use of shadow restrained, and the tactile values of woolen cloth and brocade are exceptionally vivid. Van der Weyden's great achievement here is to have created truly sculptural figures which, although motionless, have been captured in the middle of a gesture or a movement.

The Louvre *Annunciation* is also the central panel of a triptych the wings of which are most probably not the work of Rogier. Its style is quite different from that of the *Descent from the Cross* and shows closer affinities to that of Jan Van Eyck. It even reproduces certain details familiar to us from the *Arnolfini Marriage,* including the red of the bed clothes and hangings and the carved copper chandelier. Instead of the famous convex mirror, the painting features a copper medallion glinting in the background. This is also a picture replete with symbols in typical Campin style: lily, ewer and basin for purifying water, representing the purity of the Virgin Mary; a phial traversed by a ray of light evoking the miraculous birth; an orange or "Chinese apple", fruit of the forbidden tree, reminding us of the necessity of Redemption; extinguished candles, awaiting the coming of the Light, i.e. the Word made flesh. The painting seems to have been designed to suit the Flemish taste for intimate domestic scenes, according to which painters were expected to portray religious themes in familiar bourgeois interiors. Yet, as Odile Delanda has shown, this does not

ROGIER VAN DER WEYDEN
*The Annunciation*
C. 1435, oil on wood,
86 × 93 cm (34 × 36 1/2 in).
Musée du Louvre, Paris.

*Opposite*

*The Annunciation*
Details.

*Opposite*

ROGIER VAN DER WEYDEN
*Polyptych The Last Judgement*
Detail of central panel,
*St Michael.*

*Following pages*

*Polyptych The Last Judgement*
C. 1443-1450, oil on wood,
135 × 560 cm (53 × 220 1/2 in).
Hôtel-Dieu, Beaune.

derive from any concern for the minutiae of realist detail, but from properly theological reasons[1].

The new religious tendency in Flanders at that time was the *devotio moderna*. This doctrine urged the believer to meditate on Christ's humanity, by representing it to himself in the context of his present life. In Rogier's painting, the contemporary setting, underlined by the absence of haloes, is meant to draw the viewer in so that he effectively participates in the scene before him. This is why the angel Gabriel appears before Mary dressed in an immaculate alb and magnificent brocade cope, as if he had come to celebrate mass, rather than deliver a message.

Van der Weyden painted other noteworthy pictures at about the same time. These include an astonishing *St Luke Drawing a Portrait of the Virgin*, closely based on Jan Van Eyck's *Madonna with Chancellor Rolin*. Van der Weyden uses the same cubic space as Van Eyck, with an opening supported by two columns through which the main scene opens out onto a landscape in the background, but his articulation of different planes in depth is much more precise than in the earlier painting. He also produced works drawing on the same tragic inspiration as the *Descent from the Cross*, such as the *Lamentation*, of which he made three versions. In them, the Virgin weeps as she clasps her dead son in a final embrace, while the other figures look on in silent grief. But these pictures, fine as they are, are only the first hint of the power that was to be revealed in Rogier's greatest work, the *Last Judgement* polyptych in Beaune. Together with the Van Eyck brothers' *Adoration of the Lamb*, this is one of the absolute masterpieces of the golden age of Flemish painting.

The *Last Judgement* polyptych is enormous. It is made up of fifteen panels of different sizes. It was painted by Rogier Van der Weyden and his studio for the "great hall of the poor" in the hôtel-Dieu in Beaune. This hospital was founded by the fabulously wealthy Chancellor Rolin, and his devout third wife, Guigonne de Salins, for the salvation of their souls and in the hope of storing up treasures in heaven. Work began in 1443. These were dark times indeed. Beaune had suffered greatly at the hands of pillaging soldiers who were creating havoc throughout France and particularly in Burgundy; bad harvests had been followed by famine, and the plague had also struck. The existing hospitals were unable to cater for the myriad sick and suffering. The new room was a vast open nave, with a panelled barrel vault for a ceiling, and could contain thirty canopied beds along its two long walls. The polyptych was placed at one end of this space, behind the altar, in a chapel separated from the nave by an "open-

---

1. Odile Delanda, *Rogier Van der Weyden*, Paris, 1987, pp. 33-35.

work wooden partition", through which patients could follow the divine service from their sick beds.

As long as the polyptych hung in the chapel, it was traditional to open the wings on Sundays and solemn feast days. But since it has been restored, it is now kept in a neighbouring room which is air-conditioned to prevent any further deterioration due to the heat generated by the three hundred thousand visitors who come to see it each year. The panels were sawn in half across the thickness of the wood a few years ago, and both front and the reverse are now exhibited simultaneously, side by side.

On either side of the central figures of Christ and the archangel Michael, the composition is built up on two levels. Above is a cloud of gold, on which are seated the apostles, judges

in the celestial tribunal, as well as a pope, a bishop, a king, a monk and three women. Below them is the earth, from which the resurrected souls emerge, to go either to damnation or to eternal bliss. The central panel is dominated by the son of God, seated on a semi-circular rainbow, with the Virgin Mary at one end of the arc and St John the Baptist at the other. Christ's feet rest on a sphere, symbol of the universe. With his right hand, he blesses those who are saved and with his left curses those who are damned. These two gestures are emphasized by appropriate emblems, respectively, a lily and a blazing sword. Beneath Christ stands St Michael, prince of the heavenly hosts. He is pictured as young, because he is immortal and as handsome, because he is the embodiment of divine justice. He holds in his hands a scale in which he weighs

*Below*

ROGIER VAN DER WEYDEN
*Polyptych The Last Judgement*
Detail of central panel,
*The Weighing of Souls.*
Hôtel-Dieu, Beaune.

*Opposite*

*Polyptych The Last Judgement*
Detail of left wing, The Elect.

souls. The souls are represented by two little naked figures, whose names are *Virtutes* and *Peccata*. The former kneels, overcome with delight, while the latter seems horrified and screams with terror.

The lower tier depicts the elect and the damned. They are represented by two small groups of figures. They too are naked and are portrayed on a smaller, more human scale, than the saints above them. We see them propelled inexorably towards their fate. The damned are crushed beneath the weight of their sins. They heave themselves painfully up out of the cracked dry earth, surrounded by sparks of fire and wisps of smoke. In contrast, on the opposite side of the polyptych, as one approaches paradise, flowers grow more and more abundant. In Van der Weyden's time, woman was regarded as a temptress and it was therefore more difficult for her to be saved than for a man – hence there are only two women in the group which, led by an angel, are about to ascend to heaven. It was also believed that lunatics were possessed by demons. Here, the figures of the damned are tortured and deformed by hatred and their faces distorted by madness. Gripped by a collective hysteria, they are unable to weep, but instead scream and fight, as their folly draws them on towards eternal punishment[2]. At the far left-hand side of the polyptych, paradise is represented as a gothic porch ablaze with light, the door that leads to the divine dwelling place. On the other side, hell is strangely lacking in devils. Instead, it is merely represented by a pile of dark rocks spewing flames and volcanic vapours.

The reverse of the panels of the polyptych depict the donors. Nicolas Rolin is an old man, whose nose is too long and whose hair has been cut short. Guigonne de Salins lowers her eyes and gestures with her joined hands towards her book of hours; on her head she wears a starched net veil. Behind each of them, an angel is carrying a shield emblazoned with their respective coats of arms. Rolin is facing towards an elegant imitation statue of St Sebastian executed in grey tint, as if carved from marble. His wife is looking towards another imitation statue, this time of St Anthony, who is accompanied by a young pig.

At the other end of the "great hall of the poor", opposite the *Last Judgement*, stood a statue – a real statue this time – carved out of stone. It represented *Christ Bound*, his body covered with blood, broken already, waiting for the cross to be prepared on Golgotha. The nuns would light a candle at his feet whenever a patient entered his final death throes. In this way, the "poor" would draw inspiration from the resurrection of Christ triumphant in the polyptych and would find the resignation they needed to confront death when they turned towards Christ in his suffering.

2. *Cf.* Odile Delanda, *op. cit.*, p. 69.

*Opposite*

ROGIER VAN DER WEYDEN
*Braque Triptych*
Right wing, *Mary Magdalen.*
C. 1450, oil on wood, panel
41 × 34 cm (16 × 13 1/2 in).
Musée du Louvre, Paris.

*Pages 76 and 77*

*Polyptych The Last Judgement*
Detail of right wing, *The Damned.*

The *Braque Triptych*, named after Jean Braque who commissioned it, also ranks among Rogier Van der Weyden's most celebrated works. It is a small-scale work of the kind that were set upon portable altars in the oratories of wealthy individuals. When closed, it shows the classical vanity theme, a skull and a cross. Open, it displays images of Christ in the centre and, to either side – the Virgin, St John the Evangelist, St John the Baptist and Mary Magdalen. They are represented against a landscape that is rendered down to the finest detail, with its rivers and mountains, grass and leaves so precisely drawn they could almost be counted and tiny figures visible in the distance in the streets of imaginary towns – a favourite motif of the Flemish masters. The Christ is a superb figure. Once again he is depicted as an unbending judge, from whom there radiates a dazzling, almost transparent, light. He holds the globe of the earth in his left hand and raises two fingers of his right in blessing. The finest panel, however, is that showing Mary Magdalen. She sits with her hand resting on the lid of an alabaster vase, about to spread perfume on Jesus's feet. Her face, veiled with a band of gauze, her blond hair hanging down her back in long waves, even the corselet that only partly conceals her bosom – everything about her suggests not a repentant sinner, but a young woman rightly proud of her beauty.

This is no longer the monumental art of the polyptych, but the more subtle art of the portraitist. Rogier naturally excelled in this genre, being a superb draftsman. Unlike Van Eyck, he was no realist. He did not seek to capture the particular character of his model, but instead tried to create an ideal image. This approach was very popular with his contemporaries, and brought him considerable success in this genre. He was sought after by the grandest aristocrats and prelates, as well as by the wealthy bourgeoisie, who wanted him to record and embellish their features for posterity. Yet, depending on which historian you believe in, there are only between five and fourteen authenticated portraits by Rogier that have survived to this day. I will mention only two of them here, both exceptional achievements: the *Man Holding a Book*, now in London, and the Washington *Young Woman* whose thin pale face stands out against a dark background. Several writers have also drawn attention to Van der Weyden's treatment of his sitters' hands, which he almost always painted joined together, discreetly, so as not to distract from their faces, yet quietly present, always serving to underline their serenity.

In 1450 Van der Weyden travelled to Rome. His journey does not seem to have much affected his style, save in that he thereafter adopted the half-length portrait format, which was common in Italy. He was already fifty, and was too far advanced in his art to call the elements on which it was founded into

question. Yet, his *Deposition*, in the Uffizi, is very clearly inspired by Fra Angelico's *Lamentation of the Body of Christ*, in its use of a hybrid genre not normally favoured by Northern artists. Rogier's picture – in which, as in Fra Angelico's, Christ's body is being held up, as if on display, by Joseph of Arimathea and Nicodemus – is at once a Descent from the Cross, a Pietà, and an Entombment. But although the small hillock that contains the grave is typically Italian, the landscape in the distance is a pure product of Flemish attention to detail. In retrospect, we can see that this painting constitutes an exception in his work, not a new departure. With the magnificent *St Colomba Altarpiece* painted in around 1460, he returned to the very personal manner that he had made his own, particularly in the subtle treatment of the transitions between foreground and background, and brought it to new heights of perfection. The Three Kings in the central panel symbolize the three ages of life, which is only fitting, for this masterpiece was doubtless also his final work.

*Above*
ROGIER VAN DER WEYDEN
**St Columba Altarpiece**
C. 1460, oil on wood,
138 × 278 cm (54 1/2 × 109 1/2 cm).
Alte Pinakothek, Munich.

*Opposite*
**Lamentation before the Tomb**
1450, oil on wood,
110 × 96 cm (43 1/2 × 38 in).
Uffizi, Florence.

*Following pages, left*
**St Columba Altarpiece**
detail of central panel,
**The Adoration of the Magi.**

*Following pages, right*
**Portrait of a Man Holding a Book**
Before 1437, oil on wood,
33.7 × 23 cm (13 1/2 × 9 in).
Courtauld Institute, London.

# PETRUS CHRISTUS

The little we know for certain about Petrus Christus derives from archival records dating from the 15th century. There, his place of birth is given as "Baerle", a word that has provoked much debate. There are two villages of this name, one located on the present-day Belgian-Dutch border, between Tilburg and Turnhout (Baerle-Hertog) and the other lying between Trochienne and Deinze, in what is today Belgium. Scrupulous research, however, has recently dispelled this confusion and established that it was in the latter of these two Baerles that Petrus Christus was in fact born.

The Bruges *Pooterboek* indicates that he was made a citizen of the town where he was to practise the profession of painter on 7 July 1444. For thirty years, he worked to commissions from aristocrats, burghers and ecclesiastical authorities, producing portraits, devotional images, altarpieces and at least one monumental work, a *Tree of Jesse* that was carried in the annual procession of the Holy Blood in Bruges. He married, and his son Bastin became a painter like his father. Petrus was a master of two religious fraternities: the fraternity of Our Lady of the Snow and the fraternity of the Dry Tree. He was also a member of the Bruges Guild of Painters right up to the time of his death, in 1475 or 1476. Although it was long assumed that he had been trained by Jan Van Eyck and worked in the latter's studio, the dates cited in support of this hypothesis do not fit, since Van Eyck died in 1441. It is therefore extremely unlikely that the younger man ever personally met the older master, even though after arriving in Bruges he was to complete several of his paintings and would always remain faithful to the Van Eyck tradition in his own work. It is now believed that his real master was his own father, Pierre. The unusual name of Christus apparently derived from his great skill in painting *Christus-beeld* – images of the Face of Our Lord.

*Above*

PETRUS CHRISTUS
*The Lamentation*
Detail.
Musée royal des Beaux-Arts,
Brussels.

*Opposite*

PETRUS CHRISTUS
*St Eligius in His Workshop*
Detail.
Metropolitan Museum of Art,
New York.

PETRUS CHRISTUS
*Portrait of a Young Girl*
1446, oil on wood,
28 × 21 cm (11 × 8 1/2 in).
Staatliche Museen, Berlin.

The number of surviving works that can be attributed with certainty to Petrus Christus is very small. The core of his œuvre are six paintings signed and dated by the artist, all from the period between 1446 and 1457. Two other paintings, signed and dated 1452, in the Groeninge Museum in Bruges, are clearly by his hand, even though they have been extensively restored. Between fifteen and twenty other paintings have been attributed to him, with varying degrees of confidence. As many of these paintings can be dated only very approximately, the precise chronology of his work is unknown, and much controversy and disagreement still surrounds the question of his stylistic evolution.

For some art historians, he was merely an epigone, an imitator, first of Jan Van Eyck, then of Rogier Van der Weyden and even perhaps, to a lesser extent, of the master of Flémalle. Certain scholars have gone so far as to trace his many sources back to the schools of Tournai and of Haarlem. The only concession these critics are prepared to make is that Christus possessed an innate gift for simplification and generalisation, through which he was able to create a genre that was peculiar to him, the *Andachsbild*, or "meditative painting". Other experts, however, see his œuvre unfolding in a logical manner, with each influence that came to bear upon him fully and progressively assimilated by the artist. Thanks to such scholars, the errors of judgement which had previously relegated Christus to a backwater in the history of Flemish art have now at last been repaired. Joël M. Upton, one of the leading authorities on Christus, is surely right when he maintains that the important issue is not whether the painter was influenced by any given master, but how he developed the means to express his own artistic vision and so became, in the words of one 16th century critic, *"pictor famoso in Fiandria"*.

If the quality of his work were still in doubt, a single painting, generally dated from the end of his active life, should suffice to convince even the most reticent: the *Portrait of a Young Girl* in the Staatliche Museen in Berlin. The surface has the brilliance of porcelain and the purity of the overall effect looks forward to Vermeer. The lively expression of the girl and her oblique glance, suggesting that something or someone just outside the frame has caught her attention, contrasts with the frontal composition. The pink of her cheeks and lips introduces some warmth into the face, while the pure white and brown-black of the eyes echo the underlying tones of the wall behind her. Petrus Christus's portraits were once condescendingly described as rough-hewn and stilted. Yet this young girl is surely closer to Upton's description of her: "a polished pearl, almost opalescent, lying on a cushion of black velvet".

PETRUS CHRISTUS
*St Eligius in His Workshop*
1449, oil on wood,
98 × 85 cm (38 1/2 × 33 1/2 in).
Metropolitan Museum of Art, New York.

*Following pages*

PETRUS CHRISTUS
*The Lamentation*
Oil on wood,
101 × 192 cm (40 × 75 1/2 in).
Musée royal des Beaux-Arts, Brussels.

Flemish painting excelled in the art of portraiture, bringing it to unrivalled heights of perfection. Their early mastery of oil painting predisposed Flemish painters to this genre, for oil is the ideal medium in which to render the subtle nuances of facial structure and expression. At the end of the 14th century, portraits generally showed the face in profile. The simplicity of an outline could easily be made to suggest and summarize the sitter's character, and spared the artist the much more difficult tasks of rendering the contours and texture of the flesh through light and shade and of capturing the gaze, which is so hard to describe in paint and so crucial in determining the way we read an expression. In Jan Van Eyck's work, as we have seen, the portrait progressed from showing the face in profile to a three-quarter view. In his *Portrait of a Young Girl*, Petrus Christus became the first painter to depict a sideways glance in a face seen full on. This in itself demonstrates that he was no mediocre copyist.

*St Eligius in His Workshop of Art*, in the Metropolitan Museum of Art, New York, remains to this day his best-known and best-loved painting. It shows two young fiancés who have brought the patron saint of goldsmiths a quantity of precious metal to be melted down and fashioned into rings as tokens of their love. Christus gives us an extremely detailed representation of the goldsmith's shop. Not only are there all the instruments of the trade, but also many liturgical objects, carefully arranged on shelves. There is also a convex circular mirror on the right-hand side of St Eligius's table, in an obvious allusion to the *Arnolfini Marriage*. In it we can see the reflection of a square, with a couple of passers-by. The function of this mirror, however, is very different from that in Van Eyck's painting. Whereas, on one level, it can be interpreted as a symbol of vanity or a protective talisman, it is above all an anti-theft device, which the goldsmith would have used to keep an eye on his clients, just as in a present-day bank or jewellers. Although the presence of the saint gives the work a religious dimension, this remains essentially a genre painting: that is, a representation of secular and commercial activities, a scene from everyday life.

Petrus Christus, however, was also a great religious painter, whence his name. His *Lamentation* , in the Musée royal des Beaux-Arts in Brussels, for instance, is a work of exceptional beauty and aesthetic rigour. In the centre of the composition, Joseph of Arimathea has spread out a shroud on which Christ's body lies. Nicodemus holds the body up, turning it slightly to face the viewer, while the Virgin is supported in her grief by St John and Mary, the wife of Clopas. On the far left-hand side is Mary Magdalen, kneeling, and on the far right, a weeping couple, who may be Mary Salome and her husband Zebediah.

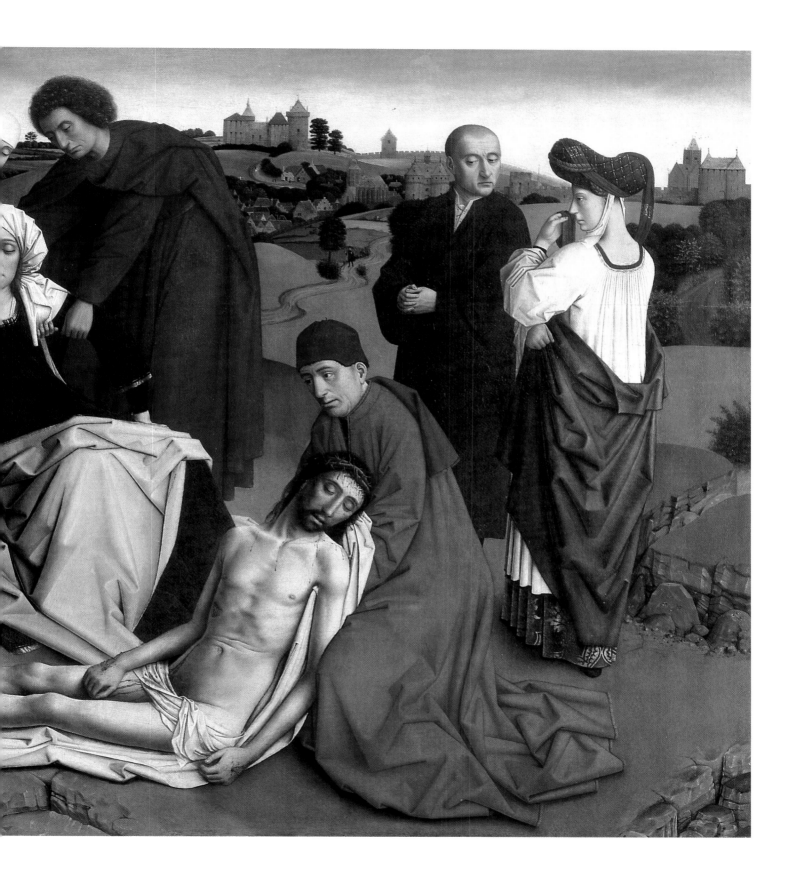

The painting is a tour de force, notable for its strong composition and economy of means. It is not only the figures which are remarkable, but also the landscape in which they are set and which stretches across the full width of the panel, with its sharply drawn stones, austerely geometrical buildings and occasional tree, as well as the still life in the foreground with its cloth, polished nails, hammer, pliers and ointment pot.

Panofsky said that Petrus Christus reduced figures and objects to "simple volumes, cast-iron blocks that are fitted into space like molten metal into its mould". And indeed, this *Lamentation* has the cold reverberation of grey steel. In Charles de Tolnay's opinion, Christus's œuvre "corresponds to that of

Piero Della Francesca" in Italy. This comparison is justified not only by the inherent quality of Christus's magnificently architectural art, but also by the keen interest in perspective which he shared with Piero.

Another painting in which Christus seems to have been preoccupied with problems of perspective is the *Virgin and Child in a Gothic Interior*. For some of his admirers, this is the artist's finest single work. The articulation of the different planes, the opening out of space through the windows along one side, the receding corridor which gives the picture depth are all of a perfection which looks forward to Pieter de Hoogh and Vermeer. The use of symbolism which he had learned from his master, Van Eyck, is again omnipresent. As in the *Arnolfini Marriage*, an orange on the window-sill to the left of the composition reminds us of paradise which was lost through the fault of our first ancestors and which has been found again only through Christ and Mary, the new Adam and Eve. The design of lilies carved along the top of the panels behind the bed are one emblem of the Virgin, as is the enclosed garden that is visible through the window. Again, as so often in the work of the first great Flemish artists, this painting is everywhere informed by the desire to show how the sacred has become incarnate in everyday life.

*The Madonna of the Dry Tree*, however, belongs to a different genre altogether. Mary is here represented surrounded by the branches of a tree like a gigantic crown of thorns. This is the tree of the knowledge of Good and Evil which, according to legend, withered at the Fall and was only brought back to life by the Virgin. The "A"s that hang from the tips of the branches are those of the first word the angel spoke to her – *Ave* – the word by which the salvation of man was begun. This devotional image is hardly much larger than a postcard, and its size may explain why, instead of a perspectival space, the figures are set against a plain black background.

Many innovations have been attributed to Petrus Christus, besides those he made in the genre of portraiture. He was, for instance, the first painter to represent the Virgin alone in a landscape setting. His most radical contribution to the progress of his art, however, was certainly the role he played in developing the depiction of three-dimensional space using linear perspective. He was, in fact, the first Flemish master to learn how to use this technique correctly. Fortunately, art historians have been able to resolve the problems of dating and attribution posed by his surviving works. Thanks to their research, Petrus Christus's place among the great masters of his age is now secure.

*Opposite*
PETRUS CHRISTUS
*Virgin and Child in a Gothic Interior*
1460, oil on wood,
71.5 × 52.1 cm (28 × 20 1/2 in).
Nelson-Atkins Museum of Art,
Kansas City.

*Below*
PETRUS CHRISTUS
*Madonna of the Dry Tree*
1444, oil on wood,
14.7 × 12.4 cm (6 × 5 in).
Thyssen-Bornemizsa Collection,
Madrid.

# WORTHY
# SUCCESSORS

After the foundations of Flemish art had been laid at the beginning of the century, other painters soon emerged to carry on the tradition of their masters. Van Eyck's peculiar serenity did not find many followers, but the clarity of his compositions, derived from the mediaeval art of illumination, was highly influential.

This second generation of artists brought to their work a new seriousness and a heightened emotional tension. They did not court variety for variety's sake but multiplied different expressions and poses in order to render the complex truth of the religious scenes they portrayed. Although their compositions were often very complicated, they made sure that there was no space simply left empty, no element that did not serve some expressive purpose. From Dieric Bouts to Hugo Van der Goes, their aim was to explore and transcribe the inner feelings of the human soul. Landscape was no longer the conveniently fictitious decor of an action, but an atmosphere, an emotional space from which the event proceeded. Perspective was now understood and applied, simply, yet with rigour. Above all, religious emotion was henceforth the central subject of art, to be expressed in all its diversity, whether as adoration, reticence or devotion.

These artists still worked in the pure Flemish tradition of attention to reality, but they were also open to the influence of Italian humanism. This was the milieu in which Justus of Ghent was immersed during his stay in Italy, where he at last initiated the local painters into the mystery of oil painting which had, hitherto, been an exclusively Flemish technique.

DIERIC BOUTS
*The Justice of Emperor Otto III.*
Right wing, detail of *The Ordeal by Fire.*
Musée royal des Beaux-Arts, Brussels.

# DIERIC BOUTS

Dieric Bouts has sometimes been referred to simply as a portrait painter, so exceptional were his achievements in this genre.

His *Portrait of a Man*, in the National Gallery in London, dated 1462, is an absolute masterpiece for example. Although relying entirely on harmonic variations of brown, incorporating tints of pink or mauve, Bouts here went as far, perhaps, as it is possible to go in the exploration of the human face. His drawing is always rigorous and self-assured. Here, he uses it to accentuate the articulation of the hands, emphasizing the veins and lines. Yet his passion for psychological truth did not prevent him from pursuing other, higher aims at the same time, as if he meant to prove that grasping the complex reality of an individual necessarily brings us face to face with the essential enigma of the divine. His religious paintings are all imbued with a sense of metaphysical mystery, as are his justice scenes. Together with his portraits, these works establish Bouts as one of the major artists of 15th-century Flanders.

Bouts came from the Northern Netherlands. He would seem to have been born in Haarlem, but no documentation has survived to prove this. What we do know for certain is that he worked in Louvain and that a certificate issued by that town on 12 July 1476 describes him as being of foreign origin: *"nativi ex patriam"*. We do not know when he was born, only that it must have been some time between 1410 and 1420. Nor do we know who his masters were, though the influence of Rogier Van der Weyden is so clearly visible that it seems likely he may have worked in Rogier's studio in Brussels.

He married Katherina Van der Brugghen, the daughter of a rich Louvain family, no later than 1448. She bore him four children. The two boys, Dieric II and Albert, were later to become painters like their father. The name of Bouts is first recorded in

*Above*

DIERIC BOUTS
*Triptych of the Virgin*
Right wing, detail
of *The Annunciation.*
Museo del Prado, Madrid.

*Opposite*

DIERIC BOUTS
*Portrait of a Man*
1462, oil on wood, 31 × 20 cm (12 × 8 in).
National Gallery, London.

*Opposite*

DIERIC BOUTS

*The Entombment*

C. 1450, distemper on flax canvas
90.2 × 74.3 cm (35 1/2 × 29 1/2 in).
National Gallery, London.

the Louvain archives in 1457. Thenceforward, it reappears in connection both with the purchase or inheritance of property and with commissions for various paintings. From this very first mention, Bouts is described as a painter: *"Dieric Bouts schildere"* (1457), for example, or *"Theodorum Bouts pictor ymaginum"* (1458).

The fact that nine years elapsed between his marriage and the first mention of his name in the city records at Louvain has led certain historians and biographers to suggest that Bouts returned to Haarlem during this time, where they see him exerting a certain influence on the Northern school of artists. Yet the available facts hardly lend credence to this hypothesis. Why would Bouts have left Louvain, a town that was just then enjoying a period of rapid economic and social expansion, and where the arts had wealthy patrons ready to hand in the person of the Dukes of Burgundy? Moreover, he had just married a young girl of that city, who had brought with her a substantial dowry. Why, in these circumstances, should he think of returning to a northern town, where the political and economic climate was still so unstable? What could he have found there to tempt an artist who had once tasted the charms of Flanders?

In late 1468 or early 1469, Bouts was appointed "official painter of the town of Louvain". He was widowed, and remarried in 1473, taking as his second wife one Elisabeth Van Voshem. He died two years later, on 6 May 1475, and was buried in the Minderbroerderkerk, the Franciscan church of Louvain, which stood close by his house.

The earliest works to have been attributed to Bouts are the three panels of the *Triptych of the Virgin*, in the Prado in Madrid, and various versions of the *Virgin and Child*. These paintings are very close in style to Rogier Van der Weyden, sometimes so close as to be virtually undistinguishable. The Prado panels set the main composition within a series of grisaille arches, which are embellished with episodes from the Old and New Testaments. The main scenes are executed in a manner that derives directly from Van der Weyden, down to the very details. Nevertheless, Bouts manages to demonstrate not only his mastery of a style, but also his own nascent originality.

It is with the *Descent from the Cross*, in the cathedral at Granada, that a truly personal style begins to emerge. Here, Bouts emphasizes the stark outline of the figures with their expressively elongated torsos; the result is not the dramatic eloquence of Rogier, but a meditation on the interiority of emotion. The space around the figures is deliberately left empty so as to intensify the atmosphere of silent contemplation and draw attention to the monumentality of the images. Bouts was steeped in a mystical sense of religion. He went on to paint a *Salvator coronatus* – now

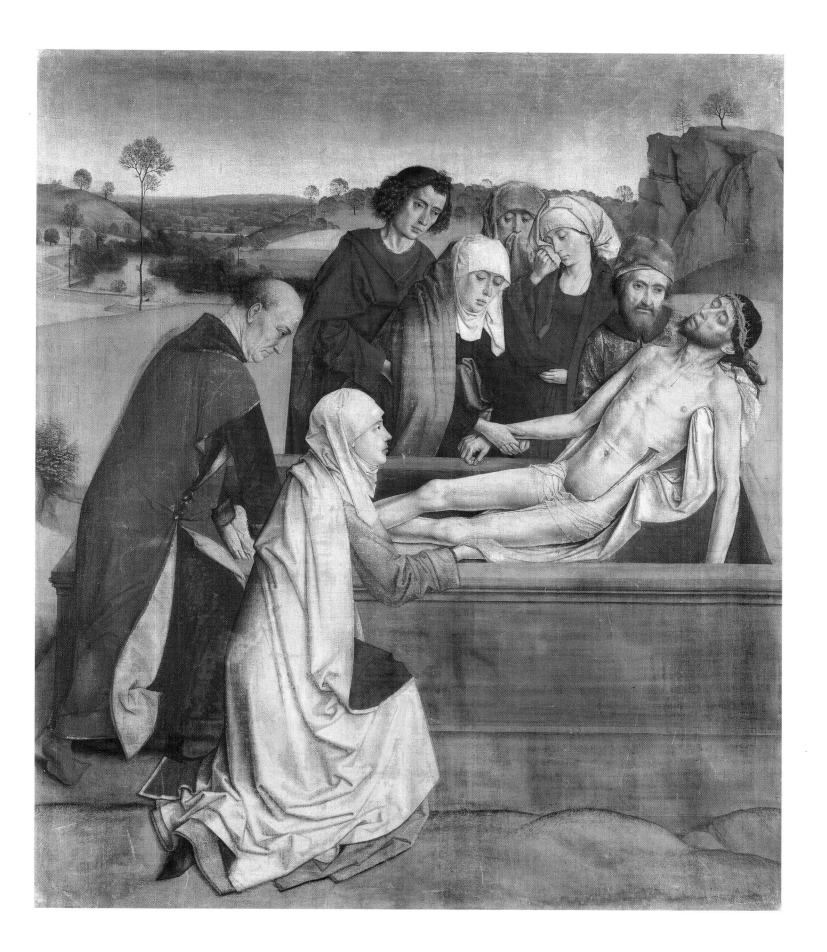

DIERIC BOUTS
*Triptych of the Virgin*
Oil on wood, 80 × 224 cm
(31 1/2 × 88 in).
Museo del Prado, Madrid.

known only from copies – in which he again drew his inspiration from Van der Weyden. But his Christ is closer to the Christ of the Rhenish mystical writer Thomas Hemerken (1379-1471) than to any of Van der Weyden's prototypes. Hemerken is generally held to be the author of the *Imitation of Jesus Christ*, a vast spiritual treatise that was one of the key texts of the *devotio moderna* movement.

In the National Gallery *Entombment*, Bouts took Van der Weyden's model and totally transformed its meaning. The folds in the cloth are heavier and more rounded, and where they break, the effect is altogether less violent. The gestures are more peace-

ful and the painting is able to transcend the pathos of the scene, so that the central emotional focus is now the intense concentration that can be read in the gazes of the different figures. Christ's head is properly ecstatic: on his brow is the crown of thorns, his eyes are closed and his mouth is half-open. The figures gathered around the tomb seem suspended between grief and astonishment. The gently rolling countryside, dotted with the occasional small tree, stretches away into the distance, its tranquility merely heightening the sense of desolation.

Besides the remarkable *Portrait of a Man*, few of Bouts's paintings can be attributed to him or even dated with any great

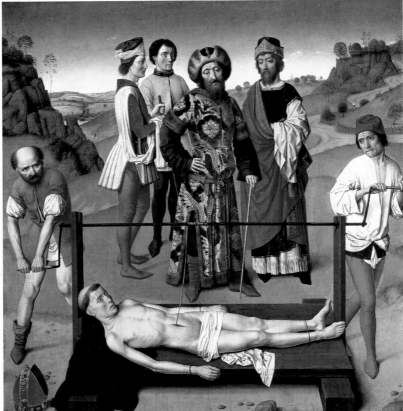

*Above*

DIERIC BOUTS
*Triptych of the Martyrdom of St Erasmus*
Oil on wood, 34 × 148 cm (13 1/2 × 58 1/2 in).
Collegiate church of St Peter, Louvain.

*Opposite*

*Triptych of the Martyrdom of St Erasmus*
Detail of central panel.

certainty. Of those that can, the three most important pieces are the *Triptych of the Martyrdom of St Erasmus*, in the collegiate church of St Peter in Louvain, the *Altarpiece of the Holy Sacrament*, in the same church, and the diptych *The Justice of Emperor Otto III*, in the Brussels Musée royal des Beaux-Arts.

St Erasmus was the bishop of Formia, near Gaeta in Italy, during the 5th century. According to legend, he was put to death by the Arian Lombards and died in the most terrible agony. Bouts represents St Erasmus virtually naked and stretched out on a board, to which he is bound by his hands and feet. A hole has been cut in his belly and one end of his intestines tied to a winch. Two executioners are busy disembowelling him. One is old and bald, and works with his sleeves rolled up, winding the handle of the winch with great vigour. The other is young; he seems to be disturbed by what is happening, and goes about his task with less enthusiasm. Behind them is a bearded figure, wearing a rich coat of blue and gold brocade trimmed with fur. He surveys the torturers with an attitude that is both simple and dignified. From the way he leans on his stick, you might think he was overseeing

some administrative formality. Of the three men with him, only one looks directly towards the scene, while the other two ignore it as if it were an event of no importance. Despite the horrific nature of the act, there is no sign of any blood anywhere. The wings of the triptych show, on the left, St Jerome resplendent in his cardinal's robes, with his emblematic lion at his feet, and on the right, St Bernard wearing a plain habit, and holding his abbot's crook in one hand.

Behind the figures, a landscape extends across all three panels of the triptych. The green hills and the roads that run between them have been identified with the rolling countryside around Louvain. The brilliance of the light and colours in which nature is rendered here is so extraordinary that one feels this must be the result of the first ever exercise in open-air painting. Bouts was a master of landscape art, as his contemporary Johannus Molanus was already aware. Even such a brutal subject as the disembowelling of Erasmus, when cloaked in Bouts's ethereal light, is invested with a certain tranquility. Nature is no longer an artificial decor, an obviously false theatrical backdrop, as it appears in 15th-century Italian painting, but an atmosphere rendered down to the finest detail, where close attention has been paid to every nuance of colour.

The central panel of the *Altarpiece of the Holy Sacrament* is given over to *The Last Supper*. It is one of the key works in the history of Flemish art. Here, Bouts breaks with the tradition according to which Christ is always represented in the act of announcing the betrayal of Judas. Instead, he chooses to show the moment at which he institutes the Eucharist. On the four side panels are biblical episodes which prefigure the sacrament, namely: *The Meeting of Abraham and Melchizedek, The Gathering of the Manna, Elijah in the Desert* and *The Feast of the Passover*. We know now that this innovation was not accidental. Two professors of theology at Louvain University, Master Jan Varenecker and Master Aegidius Ballawel, were asked to provide the painter with precise instructions as to the subjects he should represent. Work on the altarpiece began in 1464 and the painting was installed in the church four years later. A register of the Confraternity of the Holy Sacrament has survived which contains a receipt for the payment of this work, written in the hand of Bouts himself.

*The Last Supper* is remarkable for its stylistic purity and sobriety. The faces of the apostles do not vary greatly. Their gestures seem to have been frozen at a particular point in time. It is an important moment, and those present seem to be meditating on its significance. This superbly glacial and hieratic aspect of the style contrasts with other elements that are equally present, and

*Opposite*
DIERIC BOUTS
*Altarpiece of the Holy Sacrament*
Central panel, *The Last Supper*.
Collegiate church of St Peter, Louvain.

*Below*
*Altarpiece of the Holy Sacrament*
Right wing, lower tier.
*Elijah in the Desert.*

*Above*

DIERIC BOUTS
*Altarpiece of the Holy Sacrament*
Oil on wood, 185 × 294 cm (73 × 115 1/2 in).
Collegiate church of St Peter, Louvain.

*Opposite*

DIERIC BOUTS
*The Justice of Emperor Otto III*
Finished c. 1460, oil on wood,
323 × 182 cm (127 × 71 1/2 in).
Musée royal des Beaux-Arts, Brussels.

*Above*

Right wing, *The Ordeal by Fire.*

*Below*

Left wing, *The Execution of the Innocent Count.*

*Following pages*

*The Justice of Emperor Otto III*
Left wing, detail of
*The Execution of the Innocent Count.*

more down-to-earth, prefiguring the realism of a Van der Goes. Two honest servants in the far left hand corner of the room are observing the proceedings through a hatch from the kitchen. Together with another figure – who may represent the painter himself and who stands by ready to wait on Christ and his disciples – they serve to place this momentous scene firmly in the context of everyday life.

The four scenes depicted on the side panels are drawn from the Old Testament, and are more plainly narrative in character. They set small figures within vast natural landscapes. Only Elijah in the desert and the angel who bends over him with his enormous wings come anywhere near the monumental scale of the central panel.

Yet the real novelty of this extraordinary painting lies in its systematic application of the laws of perspective. Jan Van Eyck and Rogier Van der Weyden had already used perspective, but only in interior scenes that were much simpler than this *Last Supper*. They had done nothing as complex or as perfect as the architecture of this central room. Moreover, the space is not entirely enclosed, for the outside world is visible at two points: once through the windows to the left, through which distant houses are visible, and again through the arch at the back of the room. This latter opening gives onto an enclosed garden painted in blue and pink tones, as if space were stretching out across it towards an invisible horizon. The trapezoid of the white table cloth, the distribution of the figures around it and their convergence on the central figure of Christ, as well as the subtle rhythm of the different colours, all conspire to endow this complex composition with a profound pictorial unity.

The diptych *The Justice of Emperor Otto III* belongs to the genre of the justice scene. It was painted by Bouts towards the end of his life for the council room in the town hall at Louvain, which had been completed in 1460. The paintings recount the horrific misadventure that befell Otto III and his treacherous wife. Bouts had found the story in a 12th-century chronicle written by Godefroy, Bishop of Viterbo.

The Emperor had married the daughter of the King of Aragon. His wife subsequently fell in love with a count of the imperial court. When the latter refused to respond to her advances, she publically accused him of having made an attempt upon her honour. The Emperor, in a fit of anger, had the count beheaded on the spot. The count's wife asked to prove the truth of her husband's innocence by the ordeal of fire. She won her case, surviving the test unharmed. The Empress was found guilty of false accusation, and condemned to be burned alive.

Each panel of the diptych represents two successive scenes taking place in two adjoining spaces. In the first, we see the Emperor, with his crown and sceptre, and his deceitful wife, standing beside the gate of a fortified town. They are watching as the count, dressed in white, barefoot and his hands bound, is led out to his execution. Several figures, including a Franciscan monk, accompany the condemned man, who is giving his last instructions to his wife as he walks. In the foreground, we rejoin the story after the execution. The count has been decapitated, and his mutilated body lies slumped on the ground. The executioner hands the count's head to his kneeling widow, who wraps it in a white cloth. In the second panel, the Emperor is giving an audience to the widow. He sits on a throne beneath a dais, while she kneels before him to ask for reparation. In one hand she holds the livid head of her dead husband, and in the other a bar of red hot iron. The bar does not burn her, thus proving the innocence of her dead husband. Through an open doorway, we can see a hill in the background. There on a burning pyre, the Empress is punished according to her deserts.

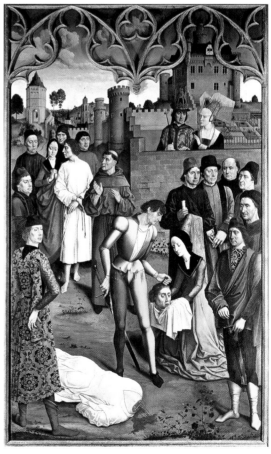

The two panels are quite different from one another, both in atmosphere and composition. In the first panel, while the victim's face is distorted with pain, those who are there to witness his death betray no sign of emotion. In the second panel, however, both the courtiers in their expensive fur-trimmed clothes and the other important personnages in their robes and red bonnets, are far from impassive. On the contrary, they are openly astonished at the miracle that has taken place before their eyes. In both panels, the vertical composition emphasizes the great height of the figures, which is a common feature in Bouts's work.

A fifth documented work by Bouts, a triptych of the *Last Judgement*, has unfortunately not survived. Two panels representing *Hell* and *Heaven*, in the musée des Beaux-Arts in Lille, were long believed to be part of this work, but recent research has shown that this is not the case.

Such uncertainties, part and parcel of the history of art, have also on occasion operated in Bouts's favour. *The Triptych of the Adoration of the Magi*, in the Alte Pinakothek in Munich, a small-scale work traditionally known as *The Pearl of Brabant*, on account of its extraordinary beauty, had for centuries been

attributed to Dieric II, Bouts's son. Now, however, it is generally agreed to be the work of the father. The faces, the poses, the landscapes are unmistakeably by Bouts himself. In the King who kneels before the Virgin, we recognize the characteristic way in which the front of the long robe is hidden beneath the bended legs, while stiff folds are depicted falling towards the ground at the rear. Another sure sign of the hand of Bouts is the way in which the figures seem to act always with a certain restraint, as if – as Panofsky puts it – the body was too foreign to the soul for there to be any interaction between them. This reticence is the distinguishing sign that unifies what would otherwise be an often disparate corpus of work, both in the size of the paintings, and in the complexity and diversity of the subjects treated.

However, such considerations should not be allowed to conceal the symbolic dimension of Bouts's work. A superb example of this is to be found in *The Justice of Emperor Otto III*. Where the decapitated body of the count has fallen to the ground, it is covered with a profusion of white flowers, heralding his innocence even before it is proved by the ordeal of fire.

DIERIC BOUTS
*The Pearl of Brabant*
C. 1470, oil on wood,
61 × 113 cm (24 × 44 1/2 in).
Alte Pinakothek, Munich.

# JUSTUS OF GHENT

The accounts of the Brotherhood of Corpus Domini in Urbino record a series of payments made between 1473 and 1475 to one Giusto da Guanto, for the execution of a painting and a banner. Vasari, for his part, mentions that in 1550 Giusto da Guanto "painted the *Communion* for the Duke of Urbino as well as other paintings". In 1604, Baldi mentioned a "Giusto Tedesco" (that is, "Justus the German" – the Italians did not distinguish at that time between the Germans and the Flemish) who, according to the writer, was the first person to introduce the technique of oil painting into Italy, in a picture he painted for the main altar of the Brotherhood in Urbino. These few indications are the only documentary evidence we have for the life and work of this enigmatic artist from Ghent.

Some historians, however, have ventured to piece together a skeletal biography as follows: Justus of Ghent – whose true name was Joos Van Wassenhove – was born between 1435 and 1440. He was made a master of the Antwerp guild of painters in 1460 and became a member of the guild in Ghent in 1464. In 1467, he was Hugo Van der Goes's patron when the latter joined the corporation. He left for Italy some time before 1473, and Van der Goes helped him to finance the journey.

Federico da Montefeltro, the Duke of Urbino, was both a distinguished condottiere and a cultivated humanist. In 1473, he decided to build an enormous new palace, for which he had commissioned a design from the Dalmatian architect Luciano da Laurana. Artists came from all over Italy – sculptors from Venice, specialists in marquetry from Florence – to work on the decoration. One room at the top of the building was intended to serve as his *studiolo* – a quiet retreat, remote from the bustle of the court, where the Duke would be able to read, write and meditate. Since

*Above*
JUSTUS OF GHENT
*St Jerome*
Detail.
Musée du Louvre, Paris.

*Opposite*
JUSTUS OF GHENT
*The Communion of the Apostles.*
Detail.
Palazzo Ducale, Urbino.

113

he could not find a painter anywhere in Italy who knew how to work in oils, he sent for a Flemish artist to decorate this private space. This artist would seem to have been Justus of Ghent.

What we do know for certain is that after Justus had painted the *Communion of the Apostles* for the Brotherhood of Corpus Domini, he went on to play a key part in the making of twenty-eight portraits of famous men for the *studiolo*. These pictures depict great philosophers, famous poets and doctors of both the Greek and Roman Churches. Today they are divided between the Galleria Nazionale delle Marche in Urbino and the Louvre in Paris. Justus was also long believed to have been the painter of the *Portrait of Duke Federico and His Son* and of *The Duke and His Son Listening To a Lecture*, which are at Hampton Court, but it is now agreed that these two paintings are clearly not his work.

Justus's style during the years he spent in Ghent was probably very close to that of Rogier Van der Weyden in his use of figures based on popular types. Skeletal bodies, forced stationary poses, and a light and subtle palette ranging from wine-red to hyacinth blue and acid green are all characteristic of his art at that period. When he moved to Urbino, he abandoned neither his earlier manner nor the Flemish concern for realism, but adapted them to these monumental works, incorporating influences from both Italian art and the humanist ideas that circulated at the Duke's court.

The portraits he executed for the ducal palace, although works of some historical importance, do not really bear comparison with the perfection in this genre of his great Italian contemporaries. Justus appears to have had assistance in his work on these paintings from certain Tuscan painters and even from Spanish artists who were residing in Urbino at the time. Some authorities have gone so far as to describe him as a mere assistant himself, attributing the true paternity of these works to Melozzo da Forli or Giovanni Santi, artists whose names are now largely fogotten, or to the Spaniard Pedro Berruguete, who – as we know – played an important role in decorating Federico's hideaway. However, the fourteen paintings in the Louvre have recently been examined using laboratory techniques, which have established that they are all drawn in a way that is typically Flemish and that two of them, the portraits of *St Jerome* and *St Augustine*, are entirely by Justus's hand.

His most important and most perfect work by far is *The Communion of the Apostles*, painted for the high altar of the Brotherhood of Corpus Domini. The picture was based on a painting by Fra Angelico that Justus may have seen at St Mark's convent in Florence, in which the disciples leave the table to kneel at Christ's

*Left*
JUSTUS OF GHENT
*St Jerome*
C. 1475, oil on wood,
117 × 68 cm (46 × 27 in).
Musée du Louvre, Paris.

*Right*
JUSTUS OF GHENT
*St Augustine*
C. 1475, oil on wood,
119 × 62 cm
(47 × 24 1/2 in).
Musée du Louvre, Paris.

JUSTUS OF GHENT
*The Communion of the Apostles*
C. 1474, oil on wood,
238 × 320 cm (93 1/2 × 126 in).
Palazzo Ducale, Urbino.

*Opposite*

*The Communion of the Apostles*
Detail.

feet. Yet, despite this influence, the finished work shows just how far Justus's style remained purely Flemish, virtually untouched by all he had seen during his time in Italy.

The scene is set in the chancel of a church built on the Latin plan, its apse supported by a row of composite columns. On each side of the painting is an opening through which distant houses and towers are visible. These panoramic views are reminiscent of Ghent or of Bruges. Christ is seen standing three-quarters on to the viewer, in front of the table. He holds the paten in his left hand, as he offers the consecrated bread to St James the Less. Around him, those disciples who have received the host appear happy and at peace, while the faces of the others express their eagerness to partake of it too. The unfortunate figure of Judas stands to one side in the shadow, as if trying to avoid Christ's gaze. In the foreground stand a plate and pitcher that will later be used to wash the disciples' feet.

In the background, to the right, is a lively group made up of Duke Federico, two of his courtiers and Caterino Zeno, the ambassador of the Shah of Persia. The presence of this

*Opposite*

JUSTUS OF GHENT
*The Communion of the Apostles*
Detail.
Palazzo Ducale, Urbino.

latter figure seems designed to indicate that the Holy Eucharist is a universal sacrament and that Christ has become incarnate in order to save all men, whatever their origins. Just behind this group a young woman can be made out, carrying the young Guidobaldo in her arms. Two angels hover above the protagonists, held in perfect balance by their tensile wings. One of them is praying, while the other simply expresses his emotion as a witness to the sacred event below.

There is a remarkable contrast between the group of the apostles, on the one hand, and that of the Duke and his followers, on the other. Justus demonstrates his great talent as a portraitist in the means he finds to express both the ardent faith of the former and the noisy activity of the latter, highlighting their facial expressions by the movement of their hands. He also plays on the contrasts between the simple, even poor clothes of the apostles, and the rich and luxurious apparel of the Duke and his companions. As for Christ, he is shown wearing a grey-blue robe. His disciples are in tunics of various colours – green, light red, yellow and brown. They have fair hair, save for one who is dark, and Judas, who has red hair. This admirable counterpoint of colours is complemented by the greeny blue of the wings of the two angels, that stands out against the dark brown of the apse. It is rare to find a painting from that period that so felicitously combines the demands of both spiritual feeling and realism.

Another celebrated monumental work was long attributed to Justus of Ghent – the *Calvary Triptych*, in St Bavo's Cathedral in Ghent. Today, however, art historians agree that of the Ghent painters of that time, only Hugo Van der Goes was capable of painting such a masterpiece. It will therefore be dealt with in the next chapter devoted to the latter painter.

Justus of Ghent has left us few documented works and the temptation is therefore to reduce his role to that of the painter who introduced oil painting into Italy. The extraordinarily rapid spread of the new technique among Italian artists would itself be enough to justify his place in history. Yet he was more than just a messenger. The Duke of Urbino's court brought together artists from all over the world, most of whom sank into anonymity, having nothing distinctive of their own to contribute to this cultural melting pot. Justus, however, was one of those who was able to absorb the artistic and humanistic values of Urbino, without thereby losing his own identity. This achievement, together with his probable role in introducing oil techniques into Italy, make the enigmatic painter from Ghent one of the most intriguing figures in European art during the second half of the 15th century.

# HUGO VAN DER GOES

Like many other early Flemish artists, Hugo Van der Goes was essentially a painter of religious subjects and portraits. He is known to have also produced allegorical and heraldic works, but none of these have survived. Both archival evidence and literary sources indicate that he was probably born in Ghent in around 1440. Nothing is known of his family, nor of his early years and his apprenticeship to his art. There is evidence that he was close to both Justus of Ghent and Dieric Bouts, but there is no way of establishing that he was apprenticed to either. From 1467 to 1475, Van der Goes is regularly cited as a member of the guild of painters in Ghent, and he served as its Dean in 1474-1475. During this period, he received many municipal commissions. In 1468 he worked on the decorations for the marriage of Charles the Bold and Margaret of York in Bruges. The following year, and again in 1472, he was involved in the ceremony of the "Joyous Arrival" of the Great Duke of the West (Charles the Bold) in Ghent. In 1474, he painted heraldic decorations for the burial chamber of Philip the Good, also in Ghent.

Van der Goes then withdrew into the monastery of the Roode Kloster in the forest of Soignes, outside Brussels, probably in 1475. He lived there as a lay brother until his death in 1482. A modest plaque on a tumble-down house can still be seen today commemorating the time he spent there. Recent archival evidence suggests that he may in fact have been born as early as 1420-1430. However, there is an abundance of information for the painter's final years, thanks to a chronicle kept during the early 16th century by one of Van der Goes's fellow monks, a man named Gaspar Ofhuys. The two had come to know each other while still novices. According to Ofhuys, Van der Goes not only continued to paint while he lived at the monastery, but retained the favour

*Above*

HUGO VAN DER GOES
*Calvary Triptych*
Central panel, detail of
*The Virgin and Companions.*
St Bavo's Cathedral, Ghent.

*Opposite*

*Calvary Triptych*
Right wing, detail of the *Brazen Serpent.*

*Above*

HUGO VAN DER GOES
*Calvary Triptych*
C. 1465-1468, oil on wood,
250 × 216 cm (98 1/2 × 85 in).
St Bavo's Cathedral, Ghent.

*Opposite*
*Calvary Triptych*
Detail of the central panel.

of the grandest burghers of Burgundian Flanders, who would travel many miles to commission works from him.

In around 1480, according to the chronicler, Van der Goes suffered a mental breakdown, and even attempted to commit suicide. Only the chants of the monks which he loved were able to calm his mind for a few minutes. Outside these rare moments of peace, he lived in a state of perpetual anxiety and depression, in which he would often try to mutilate his own body. He accused himself of countless faults and sins, and believed himself condemned to eternal punishment. Though it is impossible to be certain, it does seem that he was able to paint once again during a brief period of remission shortly before his death.

Although his working life was very short – a mere fourteen years – it was long enough for Van der Goes to establish himself as a major innovator with a powerful creative imagination. There are fifteen altarpieces and paintings by his hand that are known today. Amongst them is the *Calvary Triptych*, long attributed to Justus of Ghent. Most experts now agree that it must be the work of Van der Goes.

The central panel of the triptych depicts Christ nailed to a tall cross, with the two thieves to either side of him, tied to their gibets. They are surrounded by a crowd of figures and horsemen, and the city of Jerusalem is visible in the background. This panel is an impressive work in its own right, but the two panels to either side, which draw their subjects from the book of

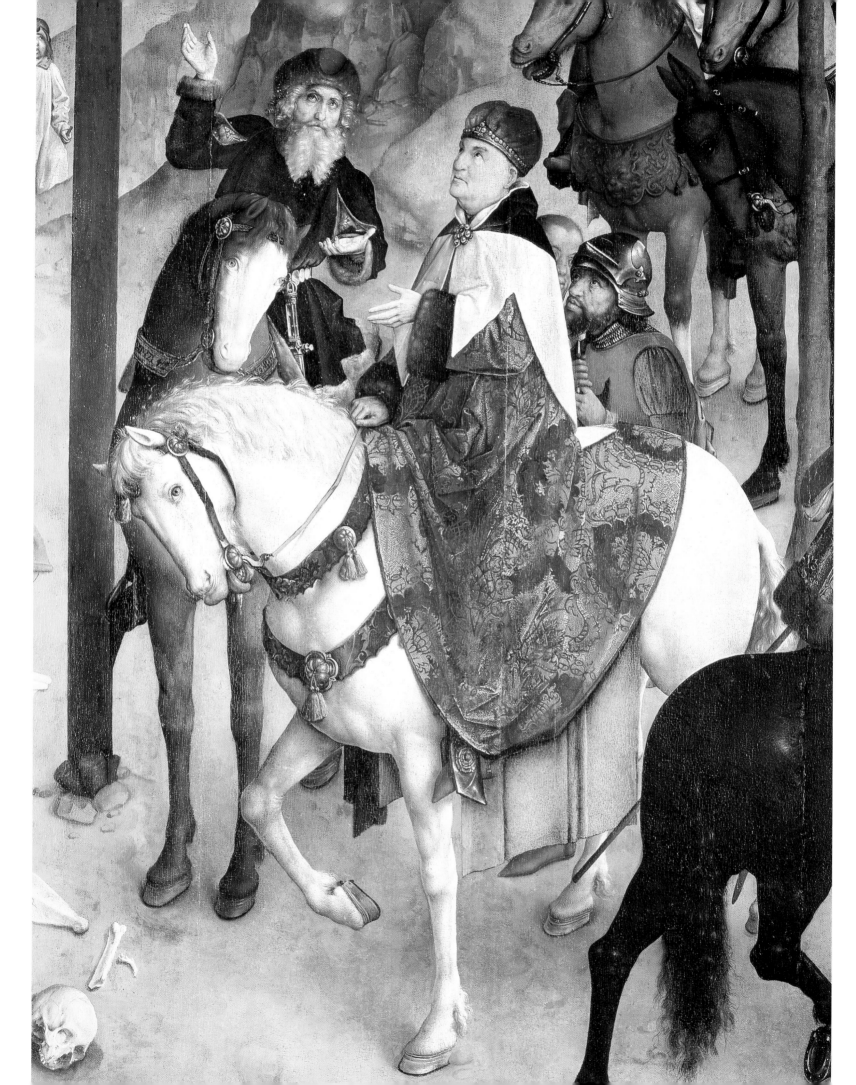

Exodus, are in many ways even finer. In the left wing, we see Moses beside a great rock that marks the limits of the foreground area. He is plunging a branch into the bitter waters of Marah to sweeten them, so that the Israelites could slake their thirst. Mothers are giving their children to drink, an old man holds out a bowl to his grandson, and another man is sipping the precious liquid from his cupped hand. The right wing depicts the episode of the brazen serpent. The people of Israel are marching through a steep-sided valley. Moses has climbed up onto a rocky promontory above them, his stick in one hand. There he complains to Jehovah that the people will not obey him any more, whereupon Jehovah turns his stick into a snake before the eyes of the astonished crowd. The people of Israel, saved by Moses, are used here to prefigure the destiny of the Christian Church, whose people have been saved by Christ.

In the background, the clouds drifting across the sky link the vast landscape into one continuous sweep stretching across all three panels. Shadows are suggested by areas of saturated colour and by the use of cross-hatching. Van der Goes's drawing is precise, taut and incisive. His palette is bright and vibrant, giving a stong sense of real open-air light. Along with more forthright tones, he delights in blending together delicate colours such as moss green and olive green, wine red, different gradations of blue, and soft pink.

Hugo Van der Goes's short career can be divided into three periods, each of which is defined by a central work: the first by the *Adoration of the Magi* – known as the *Monforte Altarpiece* –, the second by the *Portinari Triptych* – also known as the *Adoration*

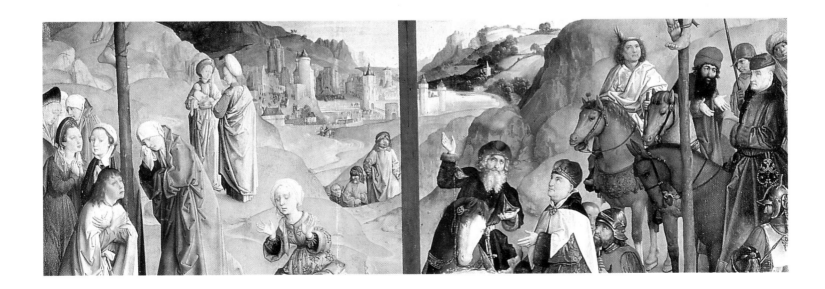

*Above*

HUGO VAN DER GOES
*Monforte Altarpiece*
C. 1470, oil on wood,
150 × 247 cm (59 × 97 in).
Staatliche Museen, Berlin.

*Opposite*

HUGO VAN DER GOES
*Calvary Triptych*
St Bavo's Cathedral, Ghent.

*Above*

Left wing.

*Below*

Detail of central panel,
*Jerusalem*.

*of the Shepherds* –, and the last by the *Death of the Virgin*. These works all testify to the artist's personal dialogue with the major painters of the preceding generation, Jan Van der Eyck and Rogier Van der Weyden, the influence of whom can be seen above all in the pictures' composition and iconography. Van der Goes appears as the heir of Van Eyck in his astonishingly detailed realism, his monumental construction of space, and the way his figures blend into an organic atmosphere of light and shade. Yet, at the same time, and from his very earliest work, he emerges as an artist with his own strongly marked personality, transposing and modifying the models he has inherited from his predecessors.

The most brilliant work from that early period is the *Monforte Altarpiece*, named after the town in which it was housed, in a college belonging to a group of Spanish Jesuits, before being subsequently transferred to the Berlin museum. It is a large-scale triptych, of which only the central panel, a long horizontal rectangle, has survived to the present day. A group of hovering angels have been amputated from the top of the panel, and the two wings have disappeared. The theme of the surviving picture is the adoration of the Magi.

The Three Kings and their followers come upon the Virgin, the Holy Infant and Joseph amid the ruins of a palace. A group of villagers observe this extraordinary scene through a gap in the wall. The figures, both actors and witnesses, are all shown on the same scale, whether humble or magnificent. They are neither reticent nor exalted, but react to the event in their various ways, surprised or self-conscious. In the background we can see a few women, some cottages and a river besides which the Kings' horses are waiting. In the foreground, symbolic flowers – the lily and columbine – and a pottery vessel are depicted with great care. A tiny squirrel is running along one of the beams above the opening through which the villagers observe the scene. Van der Goes has given free rein to his imagination, both in the composition and in his handling of paint, deploying the splendidly rich colours that are so characteristic of his art, mixing blazing reds with the most delicately nuanced shades. Nothing could be further removed from the dramatic intensity of the *Calvary Triptych* than this harmonious festival atmosphere.

Van der Goes' second stylistic phase constituted a radical break with the past, being anything but a linear development from the work of his first period. Already there are many signs of the mannerisms which were gradually to come to dominate his later work. Compared with the *Monforte Altarpiece*, many things have changed: thus, his palette is colder, mixed with much more white, and frequently including silver and gold leaf. The clothing worn by his figures is more decorative in character, emphasizing more clearly the forms of the body and setting off the faces of the saints, as well as the rougher forms of those of the angels. The contrast between areas of stasis and areas of movement in the composition is heightened and the features and poses of the figures are ever more expressive. Van der Goes chose to revive a mediaeval tradition, according to which the size of a figure varies according to their social or religious status. Thus, on the wings of the *Portinari Triptych*, the donors and their children are shown as much smaller than their patron saints. He also introduced many modifications to his technique – for instance to the methods by which he applied paint and assembled the panels.

For Panofsky, the *Portinari Triptych* had the immediacy of theatre. It was painted in response to a commission from the Florentine, Tommaso Portinari, who was the Medici's envoy in Bruges, and who later became an important banker. The left wing shows Tommaso and his two sons, Antonio and Pigello, and their protectors, St Thomas and St Anthony. The right wing shows Tommaso's wife, Maria Baroncelli, with her elder daughter Margherita, accompanied by Mary Magdalen and St Margaret. Behind them in the background are scenes that form a prelude to

*Opposite*

HUGO VAN DER GOES
*Monforte Altarpiece*
Details.
Staatliche Museen, Berlin.

the central *Nativity* – Mary and Joseph's journey on the left, and on the right, the Three Kings en route to Bethlehem. Mary, who has tired of riding, is leaning on Joseph's arm. In the right wing, we can see the Kings' servant who has dismounted to ask the way from a peasant. The presence of these background figures serves to underline the unity of the triptych, as they apparently converge, from behind the donors and saints, towards the central scene.

In the central panel, Mary and Joseph have finally come to rest under a half-ruined lean-to. This makeshift shelter is

propped up against the walls of a heavy stone building which seems to serve as a stable. They are surrounded by angels who are lost in meditation and adoration of the Child. The scene is surprising for the bare empty space in which the newborn Infant Jesus is lying, as if the painter wanted to isolate Him from the crowd of onlookers who have rushed to witness this extraordinary event. At the front of this space are a vase and a glass containing orange lilies, the symbol of the Passion, three irises, Van der Goes's favourite flower, and a few columbine stalks, the emblem of

HUGO VAN DER GOES
*Portinari Triptych*
C. 1479, oil on wood,
253 × 568 cm (99 1/2 × 223 1/2 in).
Uffizi, Florence.

*Following pages*
*Portinari Triptych*
Details of central panel.

HUGO VAN DER GOES
*Portinari Triptych*
Detail of central panel,
*The Three Shepherds.*
Uffizi, Florence.

melancholy and a common symbol of the Virgin's pains. A sheaf of corn lies flat on the ground behind these flowers, alluding to the Incarnation and the Eucharist.

Writers have often remarked on the contrast between the physical and psychological realism of the donors and their children, and the highly stylized portrayal of the rejoicing of the heavenly host. But the most provocative element of this central panel is what fully deserves to be called "the arrival of the beggars". To the right of the central space are three shepherds who are represented on the same scale as the Virgin and the saints. Their rough and rustic appearance goes beyond anything that had hitherto been seen in painting. Their faces are the faces of common men. Their heads are shaved or covered with tousled hair, their features are rugged and expressive, their skin lined, their joints and hands calloused like those of labourers who have spent their days in the fields. They have only just arrived. One of them stands, wide-eyed and open-mouthed, showing all the gaps in his teeth. He has taken off his rough straw hat, and we can sense a certain anxiety in his drawn features. The oldest of the three is already kneeling, his trowel still resting under his arm. His bag, knife and horn hang from his modest tunic which, like those of his companions, is dark green and brown. Behind them, still wearing his hat, a fourth shepherd is coming to join the group, bringing his bagpipes with him. He is dressed in lighter colours, yellowish tones of green and brown. A little further away we can just glimpse a fifth shepherd, facing at an angle to the scene.

This triptych is today in the Uffizi in Florence, where it originally hung in the chapel of the Portinari family in the church of Sant'Egidio. It is one of the largest paintings produced by a Flemish artist during the 15th century. The central panel alone measures 240 cm by 340 cm (94 1/2 x 134 in). It is larger than *The Descent from the Cross* by Rogier Van der Weyden in the Prado, and larger than the two panels of Dieric Bouts's diptych, *The Justice of Emperor Otto III*. Only *The Communion of the Apostles* by Justus of Ghent and *The Last Judgement* by Rogier are larger.

The major painting of Van der Goes's third period (between around 1478 and 1482) and very likely one of the last works he painted is *The Death of the Virgin*, in the Groeninge Museum in Bruges. The panel is almost square in shape, and the composition is similar in spirit to that of *The Adoration of the Shepherds* in Berlin. The scene is set in a totally enclosed room. The apostles are grouped around Mary's bed. The Virgin's fine blue robe contrasts with the purple sheets that cover the bed. Her livid grey face is framed by the immaculate whiteness of her wimple, and of the cushion on which her head rests. Her hands are joined, her fingers look quite bony. Her eyes have lost their lustre. She looks

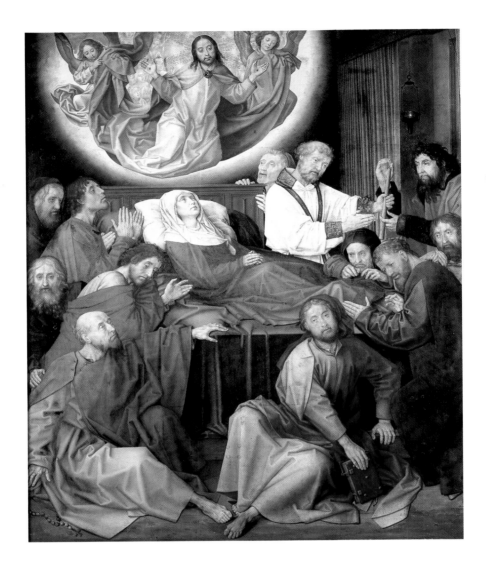

HUGO VAN DER GOES
*The Death of the Virgin*
C. 1470, oil on wood,
147.8 × 122.5 cm (58 × 48 in).
Groeninge Museum, Bruges.

*Opposite*

HUGO VAN DER GOES
*Diptych of the Fall of Man
and the Lamentation*
C. 1475, oil on wood, respectively
32.3 × 21.9 cm (12 1/2 × 8 1/2 in)
and 34.4 × 22.8 cm (13.5 × 9 in).
Kunsthistorisches Museum, Vienna.

*Above*

Left panel, *The Fall of Man.*

*Below*

Right panel, *The Lamentation.*

up one last time towards the heavens, where her Son appears to her in His glory with arms outstretched, to display the wounds in his hands. He is dressed in a blue robe and a large red cloak held up by two angels. The picture represents the moment at which life has already gently slipped away, but death has not yet completed its work.

The painter uses the apostles to ring the changes on the different varieties of grief, and their profound sadness contrasts with the detachment of the Virgin herself. Their clothes have been creased into countless shifting folds which cut across one another at right angles. Van der Goes is revealed once again as a penetrating analyst of religious feeling, of grief and devotion, and of the agitation they can cause. This work, like all those he painted during his last period, represents the eruption of sacred experience into a profane world. The artist achieves this through an abundant use of colours which strike the viewer as unreal, as if they were themselves transfigured. In this way, Van der Goes seeks to identify his painting with the mystery of transcendence itself.

To this end too, the gestures of his figures are emphatic. He uses techniques for the progressive reduction of pictorial space and the transformation of figures, which he paints half-length, not full-length. The same procedure recurs in several pictures – for instance, in the small *Lamentation*, whose protagonists are shown half-length. This painting is a variant of the *Descent from the Cross,* in Vienna, in which the figures are depicted full-length.

Unlike other contemporary Flemish artists, Hugo Van der Goes was never entirely forgotten by posterity. Over the subsequent centuries, his name is often to be found in theoretical works on art and in travellers' accounts. In 1863, the great archivist A. Wauters discovered Gaspar Ofhuys's chronicle of the Roode Kloster, which he subsequently published. The revelation of the artist's final decline into madness was ideally suited to appeal to late romantic taste, and brought about a renewed interest in Van der Goes's work. But it did so by encouraging a misleading image of the painter as an *artiste maudit* before his time, and thus as a precursor of certain modern sensibilities.

Paintings from his first two periods have often been copied and imitated, both by easel painters and by makers of illuminated books, an art that was still thriving in the late 15th and early 16th century in Flanders, Holland and France. However, his late works have found very few disciples. This fact might seem to confirm the hypothesis that his final stylistic evolution was essentially a symptom of his own incommunicable mental crisis.

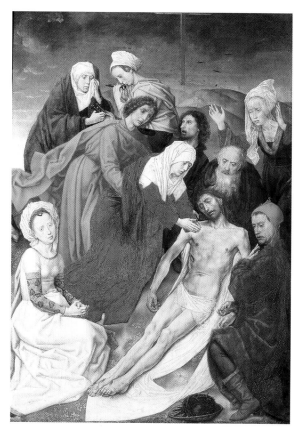

# TRADITION AND INNOVATION

The close of the 15th century saw the emergence of some of the most fascinating figures in the history of Flemish art, painters who distinguished themselves both by their talent and the diversity of their styles.

At one extreme, there was Hieronymus Bosch, one of nature's pessimists, who worked independently, in isolation from those around him. His rich aristocratic and humanist clients came to him for images of monsters which must have reminded them of the grotesque caricatures to be found in old illustrated manuscripts. At the other extreme was Hans Memling, who was known as the "Fra Angelico of the North". He continued to work in the tradition of his predecessors, tirelessly pursuing that elusive quantity, reality. In his paintings, nothing is left to chance. In his search for pictorial truth, he sought to reproduce every detail of the countless perceptual nuances he found in the world around him.

Gradually, religious subjects began to lose ground to more profane genres, which were favoured by cultivated bourgeois clients. This new market for art soon created a new generation of artists. One of their leading figures was Quentin Massys, a fine satirist, and the most Italian of all Flemish artists. He delighted in mounting critical attacks on contemporary morals. In his art, he was able to integrate the main characteristics of the Flemish tradition with the central lessons of Italian art. However, his attempts at religious painting are, alas, most often sentimental and exaggerated. His major achievement was as the precursor of the revival of genre painting that was to spread throughout Northern Europe and elsewhere during the 16th century.

HIERONYMUS BOSCH
*The Garden of Earthly Delights*
Detail of right wing, *Hell*.
Museo del Prado, Madrid.

# HIERONYMUS BOSCH

Bosch's family originally came from Aix-la-Chapelle, but had moved to Hertogenbosch, the former capital of Northern Flanders, which lies at the confluence of the Aa and the Dommel. It was this city that provided their most famous son with his pseudonym. Hieronymus Bosch was born Hieronymus Van Aecken (John of Aix-la-Chapelle). His grandfather, who had settled at Hertogenbosch where Bosch was to die in 1516, his father Antonius, his brother Goossen and three of his uncles were all painters. The date of his birth and the details of his early training can only be conjectured. His name first appears in the archives of Hertogenbosch in 1474, and in 1480-1481 he is referred to in the same source as a painter. By that date, he had already married Alyt Goyarts Van den Meervenne, the daughter of a rich burgher. The couple do not seem to have had any children.

In 1486-1487, Bosch became a lay member of the Confraternity of Notre Dame at Hertogenbosch. Exceptionally for one so young, he was accepted as a sworn member in 1488. This status was normally reserved for clerks and other worthies of the city, and thus confirms Bosch's elevated social status. He was the only "sworn painter" in the Confraternity, a fact which may also indicate that he had received an intellectual education. Isolated as a man and independent as an artist, he remained aloof from the stylistic quarrels of his day. He owed more to the tradition of manuscript illumination than to that of painting. His peculiar and absolutely innovative art seems to have been largely the product of his own unaided genius.

Bosch's principal patrons were naturally to be found among the other members of the Confraternity. These influential friends also helped him to build up a wealthy clientele among both the Spanish and the Flemish bourgeoisie. It was a Spanish

*Above*

HIERONYMUS BOSCH
*Triptych The Hay Wain*
Detail of the right wing, *The Damned.*
Museo del Prado, Madrid.

*Opposite*
*Triptych The Hay Wain*
Central panel.

HIERONYMUS BOSCH
*Triptych The Hay Wain*
C. 1490, oil on wood,
135 × 190 cm (53 × 75 in).
Museo del Prado, Madrid.

client, Felipe de Guevara, who was to become one of the painter's most important "posthumous" collectors. He eventually owned at least six pictures by Bosch, including the original version of the *Hay Wain*, now in the Prado.

The paintings by Bosch which most appealed to the bourgeoisie were those that were most typically Flemish. His aristocratic clients, on the other hand, bought mainly those works that depicted fantastic scenes full of grotesque devilish figures. It was this latter genre that was to ensure that Bosch's fame would endure after his death, and which has been the focus for the intense interest he has generated in our own century, beginning with his vogue among the surrealists.

His success during his own lifetime was in part due to the humanists' fascination with the strange, the unnerving and the occult. This essentially aristocratic milieu was already far from conventional. Its members were influenced above all by the fashion for neo-platonism that had sprung up during the preceding decades, rather than by any philosophical obsession with apocalypse. The patrons who purchased Bosch's strange works were looking not for an eschatological symbolism, but for the expression of the unconscious mind, a mysterious inarticulate universe that was still largely taboo for philosophy. Whatever psychiatrists may like to suggest, Bosch was neither mentally ill, nor seriously neurotic; but nor was he a Jan Van Eyck, whose art embodies a state of total serenity, untroubled by any doubts as to the fundamental goodness of both man and God. Bosch was the most pessimistic of all Flemish painters, and the one who gave fullest expression to the anxieties of his age.

For indeed, the times had changed. During the Middle Ages, lepers moving through the suburbs of every town shaking their rattles and beggars exposing their festering wounds in church had been regarded as normal occurrences. Now the new ruling class, the wealthy burghers, the merchants and the bankers, were growing arrogant as they grew rich. Those who had previously been tolerated, were now condemned as "deviants": whores, bandits, the drunken and the dissolute, unemployed soldiers, villeins who had suffered bad harvests and famine, the poor in all their guises, stood accused of disrupting the social order. They were seen as lazy parasites, as madmen who had to be supervised and controlled.

*The Ship of Fools,* in the Louvre, seems to have been inspired by Sebastien Brant of Basel's poem, *Das Narrenschiff.* If such is indeed the case, then Bosch's painting should perhaps be read as a vigorous satire on drunkenness, the origin of every vice. "Woe to he who sails in the ship of fools, and moves towards hell laughing and singing", wrote Brant. But it is possible that the picture is based not on Brant's poem, but on Jacob Van Oestvoren's *De blauwe Scuut (The Blue Ship),* which proposes that instead of locking up the mad – as they would be a century later – they should be dealt with more "gently", and placed together in a boat that would sail up and down for ever more on the high seas.

Ten or so figures are crammed together into a boat that is too small for them. A banner and a roast chicken have been pinned to the mast, planted in the middle of a bush. At the top of the mast is a may tree. A man armed with a knife has emerged from the bush and is trying to cut the cords that hold the chicken. To one side, three men are trying to eat a pancake that is suspended from a string. A madman, his fool's bauble in his hand, is sitting on a branch stripped of its bark, drinking from a bowl. There are two naked figures in the water, one of them hanging onto the boat. A nun is playing the lute for a monk who sits opposite her and who seems to have fallen under her spell. In the prow, a woman is lifting up a pitcher which she intends to use to strike a man who is lying stretched out on the floor of the boat. It is possible to interpret this complex scene in many different

HIERONYMUS BOSCH
*Triptych The Hay Wain* (closed)
C. 1490, oil on wood,
135 × 90 cm (53 × 35 1/2 in).
Museo del Prado, Madrid.

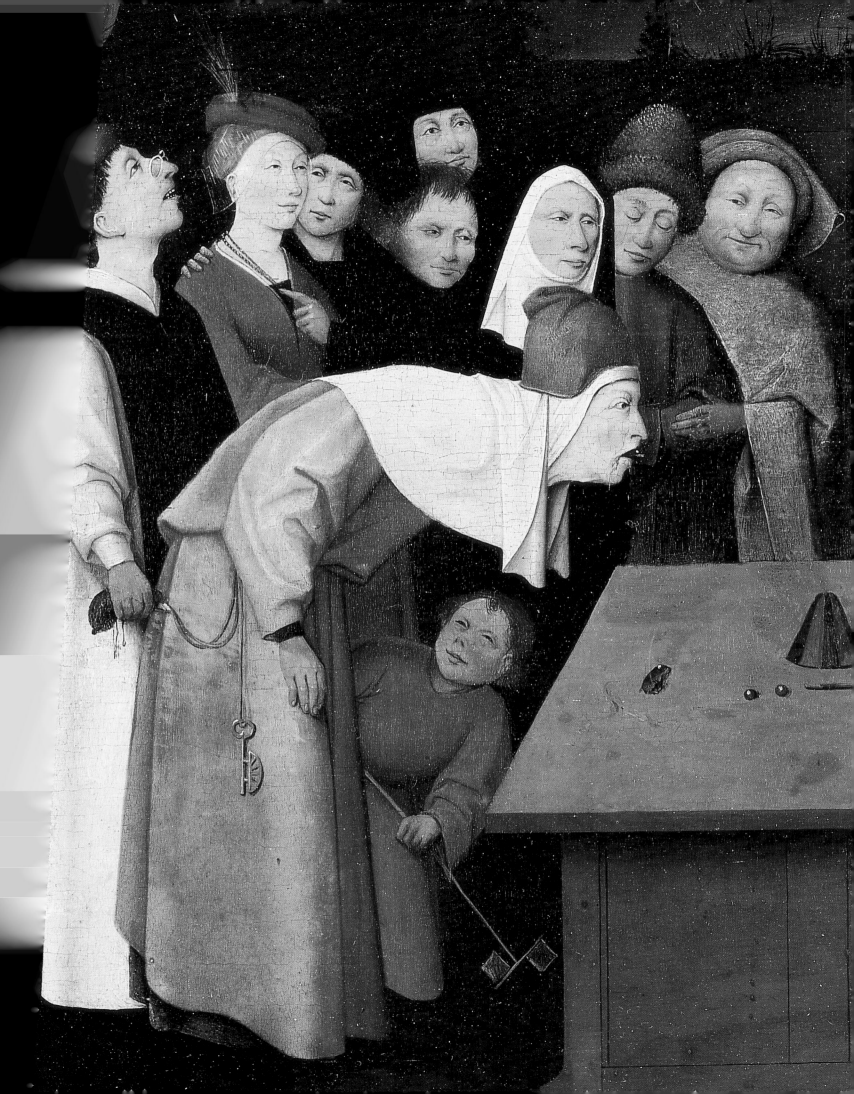

ways. But the hypothesis that *The Ship of Fools* represents unruly behaviour provoked by drunkenness would seem to be corroborated by the lower part of the picture, which has been separated from the rest, and is now in the New Haven museum. In this fragment, an obese man is sitting astride a barrel, while two characters engage in a scene of clandestine courtship, clearly intended as a prelude to fornication, which in those days was viewed as a serious crime. "The life of those who have no care is madness, they have neither compass nor rudder to guide them": that is the apparent message of this work.

*The Conjurer*, now in the museum at St Germain-en-Laye, is a caricature on naivety and trickery. The scene takes place in an ill-lit cul-de-sac, closed off by a wall with grass growing along its top. A conjurer in a long red robe and a tall black hat is demonstrating feats of léger-de-main before a tight-packed group of passers-by. In the audience is a tall man, also dressed in red and who seems to have been chosen as the fallguy of this particular manœuvre. He is so fascinated by the marble which the magician is manipulating between his thumb and forefinger, that he has bent over double. A frog has just jumped out of his mouth onto the makeshift table. Meanwhile, just behind him, a third man who is pretending to look elsewhere takes advantage of his victim's preoccupation to relieve him of the bulging purse that hangs from his belt. This genre scene was a favourite theme with painters, who enjoyed demonstrating how audiences let themselves

HIERONYMUS BOSCH
*The Conjurer*
C. 1475-1480, oil on wood,
63 × 65 cm (25 × 25 1/2 in).
Musée Municipal,
Saint-Germain-en-Laye.

*Opposite*
*The Conjurer*
Detail.

*Above*

HIERONYMUS BOSCH
*The Cure for Folly (or Stone Operation)*
C. 1490, oil on wood, 49 × 35 cm (19 1/2 × 14 in).
Museo del Prado, Madrid.

*Opposite*
*The Cure for Folly*
Detail.

*Following pages*
HIERONYMUS BOSCH
*Triptych The Temptation of St Anthony*
C. 1505, oil on wood, 131.5 × 119 cm (52 × 47 in).
Museo Nacional de Arte Antiga, Lisbon.

be duped by a charlatan's trick or a fortune teller's predictions. But in Bosch's hands, what might have been merely a good-natured joke turned into a cruelly sarcastic joke against humanity, a vision stripped of all illusions.

Bosch's treatment of the *Last Judgement* operates on similar principles. Unlike other contemporary painters, he omits the resurrection of the dead. He depicts merely a handful of the blessed and, opposite them, ranges a whole legion of the damned, who are condemned to remain on earth and suffer torment at the hands of devils. This image of an implacable God was doubtless influenced by the humanist scholars of the Rhine valley. The painter's conception of the Last Judgement is purely legalistic. Justice takes precedence over mercy. In other paintings, he dealt directly with the themes of idiocy and universal stupidity. *The Cure for Folly* (also known as *The Stone Operation*) is a burlesque on the folly of trying to turn the mad into sane men. The *Procession of the Blind*, known only from an engraving, shows a group of blind people who start out trying to bludgeon a pig to death, and who end up turning on each other.

The "vices" played a central role in Bosch's iconography. They are almost always presented as forms of stupidity or greed and are always attributed to figures drawn from the lower social orders. The principal vices represented are immodesty, violence, gluttony and drunkenness, as well as various different kinds of excessive behaviour and poverty, which are seen as the fruits of debauchery. This vision informs many of the details in his paintings and is derived from ideas that were central to 15th century literature on madness.

Bosch's greatest achievements as an artist are the three triptychs which have made him famous: *The Hay Wain, The Temptation of St Anthony* and *The Garden of Earthly Delights*.

The first of these triptychs is now in the Prado in Madrid, and there is also a copy in the Escurial. The subject comes from an old proverb: "The world is a hay wain, each man takes from it whatever he can grab." The left wing depicts three scenes: the Fall of the Angels, the Creation of Eve and the Temptation of Eve and Adam Expelled from Paradise. This last scene serves as a prelude to the vision of universal moral decadence in the central panel, where a crowd of people are mobbing a hay wain carried by a cart. On the right wing is a vision of the hell and the glimmering flames that await the figures from the central panel after they have been judged. The cart is drawn by figures representing the "vices" and by devils. The composition is crowded with different figures. A pope, an emperor and princes in their finery follow the cart on horseback. A crowd, to judge from their apparel consisting mainly of beggars, gipsies and Jews, is milling

*Above*

HIERONYMUS BOSCH
*Triptych The Temptation of St Anthony*
Detail of central panel.
Museo Nacional de Arte Antiga, Lisbon.

*Opposite*
*Triptych The Temptation of St Anthony*
Detail of central panel.

round the cart and everyone is trying to fight their way up onto it so they can make off with a little hay. Those who are repelled fall back under the wheels and are crushed. Meanwhile, on the top of the hay wain, two carefree lovers are making music, apparently oblivious to what is going on around them. In the clouds above, the figure of Christ appears, his face infused with pain and sympathy for humanity as it struggles on towards its own damnation. On the back of the wings, two scenes depict the story of the *Prodigal Son.*

There have been many different interpretations of this triptych, but all agree on one crucial aspect: the painting expresses the vanity of worldly scheming and trickery, the futility of the violent struggle to lay hold of ephemeral goods, in which people wear themselves out trying to obtain their share. Those who take part in this competition are stumbling madly and blindly towards eternal damnation.

*The Temptation of St Anthony,* in the Museo Nacional de Arte Antiga in Lisbon, is apparently based on a short episode in the *Golden Legend* by Jacques de Voragine. The text serves as a pretext for the painter to imagine a veritable sabbath in which fish, pigs and various kinds of animals are seen to take on human forms, and he responds by covering the canvas with allusions to lust, prositution and sodomy, while bodiless monsters made up entirely of a head and a leg plunge headlong into the celebration

*Above*

HIERONYMUS BOSCH
*Triptych The Garden of Earthly Delights*
C. 1505, oil on wood, 220 × 389 cm (86 1/2 × 153 in).
Museo del Prado, Madrid.

*Opposite*

*Triptych the Garden of Earthly Delights*
Details of left wing, **Paradise.**

*Following pages*

*Triptych The Garden of Earthly Delights*
Detail of central panel.

*Pages 156 and 157*

*Triptych The Garden of Earthly Delights*
Detail of right wing, **Hell.**

of a black mass. The horror of these activities stands in powerful contrast to the steadfast soul of the saint, whom the devil is unable to tempt out of his composure. This painting is typical of Bosch's fantasies. It shows how his imagination was always fertile in inventing both new metamorphoses of the visible world, and new torments for its inhabitants.

*The Garden of Earthly Delights*, in the Prado, has also given rise to many different interpretations. For some, it is a satanic comedy, for others a sensual dream. Yet perhaps the most penetrating analysis is that proposed by Wilhelm Fraenger, a German historian. It is no exaggeration to say that Fraenger's remarkable book on Bosch has completely changed the way we now approach his art.

For Fraenger, this famous triptych is a profoundly religious work. It was not intended to be hung in a church, however, but was painted for a secret, non-violent heretical sect, known as "The Brothers and Sisters of the Free Spirit". The adepts of this movement were inspired by the myth of the androgyne, whose *locus classicus* is in Plato's *Symposium*. According to the myth, there was a time when human beings each contained within themselves both a masculine and a feminine principle. They were cut in two and condemned to live as incomplete beings by Zeus, who was outraged by the attempt they had made to scale Mount Olympus. The Free Spirit sect believed in a spiritual erotics, the archetype for which was the innocent love of Adam and Eve before the Fall. They considered woman to be man's equal and not an object of contempt as in Catholic doctrine, where she was commonly described as "Satan's door". They preached the union of souls in the flesh, and there was even one famous woman member who, according to several different witnesses, could impart more spiritual wisdom in a few nights, than could be obtained through many years of theological study.

Seen in this perspective, the triptych is no longer baffling and obscure, but a work of limpid clarity. On the left wing is the Garden of Eden, with the eternal fountain and the Tree of Life. It is filled with many innocent animals – giraffes, elephants, unicorns, giant lizards and whole flocks of birds. Adam is presented as an Apollonian god. He is united with Eve whom he holds by the wrist in this dawn of Creation. In the centre is the millenial kingdom and the fountain of eternal youth. A Dyonisian bestiary of animals, exotic, mythical and domestic, mix and mingle with human figures as they race round the Pool of Life in a triumphal round driven by the power of the sexual instinct. On the right wing is hell, a place of temporary trials and afflictions, played out against a fiery background. The cosmic tree is covered with moss, the cosmic egg is rotten and burst, the cosmic ocean has frozen over, and the boat of time has hoisted all its sails in vain as it lies ice-bound.

*Opposite*

HIERONYMUS BOSCH
*Triptych The Garden of Earthly Delights*
detail of right wing, *Hell.*
Museo del Prado, Madrid.

In this triptych, Bosch takes us back to the beginning of the world, when sin did not yet exist – and never would have, had it not been for the disastrous doctrines of the Catholic religion. This reading would seem to be supported by the reverse of the wings which, when closed, depict the virgin Creation on the third day, when rain fell over the dry ground and gave birth to the first plants.

Fraenger's insight has allowed him to interpret even the most hermetic of the painter's extravagant inventions. In the past, these have often been attributed to his madness, but now turn out to have each a precise symbolic signification. Thus the men and women who are associated with gigantic fruit, emblems of the earth's fertility, or who bend over flowers in bloom, or carry enormous blackberries, or who try to penetrate the flesh of huge pumpkins, are groups of lovers. The figures that are imprisoned in a spherical seed represent love's alchemy. A solitary recumbent figure lying with legs strangely spread in the form of an upsilon and sex concealed out of fear and false modesty, is a symbol of masturbation. The men who, having taken a bath to purify themselves, are seen marching joyously towards Leda's egg, illustrate the different stages in the soul's gradual progress towards higher values and aims. On the right wing, the musicians who are spiked on their instruments or deafened by them, are minstrels who have misunderstood their art, and who have debased music, the royal consort of the Cosmos, dragging it down to serve the profane world. The arguments I have rather brutally summarized here, are explained in all their many ramifications in Fraenger's magisterial analysis.

Bosch was buried in 1516 at the age of sixty-six with the full honours of the Church. This does not in itself rule out the possibility that this rich, well-known and, in appearance at least, conventionally pious artist was in fact a secret follower of the "Brothers and Sisters of the Free Spirit". He was certainly able to interpret their doctrines fluently in paint, as if he were intimately acquainted with them. Yet ultimately, there is no way we can really be certain one way or the other. The sect was heretical. Its members were bound by oaths of secrecy, and those whose identity was revealed were invariably burned at the stake. Yet, if Bosch did paint a few hermits, he showed relatively little interest in conventional biblical scenes, which he tended to render without any great feeling. This is not in itself concrete proof, but it is perhaps enough to give us pause for thought.

# HANS MEMLING

Until the middle of the 19th century, Memling's biography inhabited a mysterious world of legend that had been invented by certain Flemish writers, and was later heavily influenced by romanticism. With the discovery of archival material which at last provided a few hard facts concerning his origins, his marriage, his children, his possessions, his patrons and his death, all this changed. We now know that Memling came from Germany, being born in Seligenstadt, a town on the river Main near Frankfurt, in around 1440. In 1465, he is mentioned in the register of the burghers of Bruges, although not in the register of the painters' guild of that city. He never held administrative office, which suggests that his position must have been in some way a privileged one. He had married a woman called Anna de Valkenaere, by whom he had three children, and they lived together in St George Street in a large house, of which he later became the owner. He died on 11 August 1494, and was buried in his adoptive town, in the cemetery of St Giles' church.

Despite his German origins, his name was very soon linked with the artistic milieu of Bruges. Memling worked for the local burghers, for guilds and convents. Above all, he did a great deal of work for the hospital of St John, now a museum where many of his paintings hang. Contemporary chronicles and stylistic analysis together have been able to provide a few clues as to his training. It seems possible that between 1455 and 1460 he was in contact with the Cologne school of painters. Vasari mentions him as a "pupil of Van der Weyden", and indeed, his treatment of figures and of composition do suggest that Memling had a profound knowledge of Rogier's work. It is even possible that he was still a member of his studio at the time of the master's death, in 1464. In addition to his monumental works, many small-format

*Above*

HANS MEMLING
*Triptych of St John the Baptist
and St John the Evangelist*
Detail of right wing.
St John's Hospital, Bruges.

*Opposite*

*Triptych of St John the Baptist
and St John the Evangelist*
Detail of left wing.

*Above*

HANS MEMLING
*Triptych of St John the Baptist
and St John the Evangelist*
C. 1479, oil on wood,
173.6 × 331.5 cm (68 1/2 × 130 1/2 in).
St John's Hospital, Bruges.

*Opposite*
*Triptych of St John the Baptist
and St John the Evangelist*
Detail of central panel.

paintings by Memling have survived, several representative examples of which can be seen in the Hospital of St John in Bruges.

Memling followed tradition in taking his subjects from the Bible and the lives of the saints. In addition, there are twenty-five surviving portraits by his hand, most of them half-length. He borrowed many of his figures and compositions from Van der Weyden, and his originality lies in the way he tempered their dramatic intensity, reorienting them towards a pervading sense of balance and calm. The figures are given pure simple forms, using weak contrasts of light and shade to define outlines and suggest volume. Memling often arranges them geometrically, as for instance in *Sir John Donne of Kidwelly Triptych*, or the *Triptych of St John the Baptist and St John the Evangelist*. He often re-employs the same formula, whatever the situation, even when the figures are standing in a landscape, as in the *St Chistopher Triptych*. A similar quest for an integrated spatial unity is visible in the *Calvary Triptych* and in the *Passion Panorama,* in which numerous figures and small groups are carefully distributed throughout the space.

This search for spatial organization often took an empirical form. Architectural and landscape elements are used to structure the space and divide it up according to sometimes "archaic" principles. Yet it does appear that Memling was well acquainted with aerial perspective and with some of the principles of central

HANS MEMLING
*Sir John Donne of Kidwelly Triptych*
C. 1475, oil on wood, 70.5 × 131 cm (28 × 51 1/2 in).
National Gallery, London.

perspective, which was based on mathematics and Euclidean geometry. Nor was he simply reappropriating the analytical procedures of Jan Van Eyck, though he did share his humanist committment to attention to the surrounding world and, like Van Eyck, would concentrate on the rendering of textures and colours, and the reflection and refraction of light. His work is also remarkable for his close observation of plants and animals. His figures' poses are always characteristic, as are his backgrounds, for which he was constantly inventing new nuances of detail and approach: an interior flooded with light, or a landscape executed in deliberately brilliant tones. Throughout his work, Memling shows little

sign of any evolution in his style. He continued to repeat figures and compositions right up to the end, though in his last years he did borrow some decorative elements from the art of Lombardy, as can be seen in *The Virgin with Child in Majesty between Two Musicians*, now in the Uffizi.

His care for detail and constant concern for harmony are part of his predilection for a classical style. These aspects of his art are given their finest expression in his most famous work, the *St Ursula Shrine*. Memling was commissioned to decorate a new reliquary, to which the saint's remains were to be transferred on 21 October 1489 during a grand ceremony in the chancel of

HANS MEMLING
*St Ursula Shrine*
1489, gilded and painted wood,
87 × 33 x 91 cm
(34 1/2 × 13 x 36 in).
St John's Hospital, Bruges.

*Opposite*
*St Ursula Shrine*
End panel.

*Following pages, left*
*St Ursula Shrine*
Detail of Scene I, side panel.

*Folowing pages, right*
*St Ursula Shrine*
Detail of scene III, side panel.

the church of the hospital of St John. (The relics would seem to have previously been kept in a small 14th century chest, which has also survived).

The new shrine was made of wood, based on a model in precious metal. It is in the form of a house or chapel, the pack-saddle roof of which is set with painted trompe-l'œil *tondi*. The decoration of pinnacles, gables, crockets, finials, interlacing and statuettes in niches, is in the finest flamboyant gothic style. The six arched openings in the sides take the place of stained glass windows, and recount six episodes from the life of the saint as recorded by Jacques de Voragine in *The Golden Legend*. Ursula was a Breton princess. She agreed to marry Eree, son of the pagan King of England, on the condition that he convert to Christianity. She was subsequently martyred for her faith at the hands of the Huns.

Memling begins with the first stage of Ursula's journey along the river Rhine, which brought her to Cologne. Helped by a few of the eleven thousand virgins who accompanied her, Ursula is disembarking from their boat, while sailors remove her luggage from the hold. In the distance, two windows give onto the young girl's bedroom where, while she sleeps, an angel appears to tell her of her impending martyrdom. In the next picture, the fleet, represented by two ships, casts anchor at Basel and the pilgrims leave the city to continue their journey over the Alps on foot. After crossing the mountains, they arrive at Rome, where they are received by Pope Cyriac, who is surrounded by various Church dignitaries. The pope and his followers having decided to accompany the future martyrs on their return journey to Cologne, we next come upon them in Basel. The last two scenes are devoted to the massacre: Eree is murdered in the arms of Ursula, and as she refuses to marry the son of the King of the Huns, the King kills her with an arrow through her heart. On one end of the shrine is St Ursula, arrow in hand, with ten of the eleven thousand virgins sheltering beneath her robe, and on the other, the Virgin and Child with two kneeling nuns. Each of these scenes is set in a chapel which suggests an imaginary interior for the reliquary.

Dirk Devos, the leading modern expert on Memling, has related how thoroughly the artist researched this work, visiting the places that he was to paint in order to get the buildings exactly right. The Rhine itself acts as a unifying thread running through the different episodes in the cycle. "On one side of the reliquary", writes Devos, "the ships are coming from the north, and cast anchor on the left bank, so that the town is on their right. On the other side, the ships are sailing towards the north, running along the right bank as they advance downstream, and thus the city is to their left. Everything is so finely observed, that one can

*Above*

HANS MEMLING
*Triptych The Last Judgement*
Bef. 1472, oil on wood
Muzeum Narodowe, Gdansk.

*Opposite*

*Triptych The Last Judgement*
detail of central panel.

*Following pages, left*

*Triptych The Last Judgement*
Left wing.

*Following pages, right*

*Triptych The Last Judgement*
Detail of right wing, *The Damned.*

reconstruct the angle from which the artist viewed the city with great precision, proof that Memling really did make drawings from the viewpoints he had chosen for his pictures of the ships at rest on both legs of their journey."[1] Rarely has an artist gone further in the pursuit of pictorial truth, a feat that is all the more astonishing given the very small size of the pictures.

But this almost obsessional concern for realistic detail did not prevent Memling from using allegory and symbol in his work. In one of his early works, the *Last Judgement Triptych*, the damned and the elect are linked together to form a garland of bodies, some tortured, some beatific, in descending and rising forms that span the entire composition. Christ is seated on a circular rainbow which separates the world above from the world below, his feet resting on a golden globe. To either side of his head are the lily of mercy and the blazing sword of justice. The *Allegory of Chastity* is another quite astonishing painting. A young girl stands chastely inside a huge block of amethyst, protected by

1. *Cf.* catalogue de l'exposition *Memling*, Bruges, Groeninge Museum, 1939, p. 142.

*Above*

HANS MEMLING
*Allegory of Chastity*
Oil on wood,
36 × 29 cm (14 × 11 1/2 in).
Musée Jacquemart-André, Paris.

*Opposite*

HANS MEMLING
*Triptych of Earthly Vanity and
Divine Salvation*
Two of the three panels

*Vanity* and *Hell*
C. 1485, oil on wood, each panel
22 × 14 cm (8 1/2 × 5 1/2 in).
Musée des Beaux-Arts, Strasbourg.

two lions wearing shields. The picture is clearly intended as an allegory of virginity and purity as the path that leads to eternal life. The *Triptych of Earthly Vanity and Divine Salvation* is made up of three panels, all three of which are painted on both sides. This reversible painting would seem to have been intended for use as an aid to private meditation. When the panels are folded slightly inwards, the triptych will stand unsupported – for example, on a table. Its symbolism centres on the opposition between Good and Evil. A woman wearing a diadem in her long hair, with a griffon and two greyhounds at her feet, and a mirror in her hand in which she contemplates her naked image without shame, represents vanity and lust. To one side of her is Death, whose genitals are masked by a toad, the satanic animal *par excellence* and, to the other, an androgynous devil. Each of these figures bears a premonitory sentence.

Memling was one of the central figures during these closing years of the century of Early Flemish art. He belongs with the painters who laboured, at the height of the Golden Age of Burgundian rule in Flanders, to represent the reality of the world in paint. He worked in Bruges during what was still a privileged period, as did Quentin Massys. Great Burgundy, the "Duchy of the West", still shone then with the last rays of its magnificence. One anonymous contemporary wrote of Memling: "He was for a short while the greatest painter in the whole of Christendom."

Then came silence and neglect, until the beginning of the 19th century, when he was rediscovered by the philosophers and poets of German romanticism. They identified him with their conception of the Christian ideal, and baptised him the "Fra Angelico of the North". F. von Schlegel was an enthusiastic admirer of this "Flemish Burgundian who was born on German soil". His friends, the Boisserée brothers, hunted down Memling's paintings. It is largely thanks to these enthusiasts that he is today one of the most popular of the Old Masters, whose art is again able to speak to a wide public.

# QUENTIN MASSYS

Quentin Massys was without any doubt the most important painter working in Antwerp in the first quarter of the 16th century. Historians have divided his work into three principal genres: religious works, moralizing genre pictures and portraits. There is no sound evidence for the hypothesis that he was a blacksmith and medal-maker, which probably stems from a confusion between him and his father, Joos, or a brother who shared his father's name. Nor is there any document that can be cited to support the theory that he worked as a tapestry designer. It seems possible that he trained as a painter in Louvain, perhaps with one of the sons of Dieric Bouts, Albert or "Dieric the Younger". It also seems likely that he was acquainted from an early age with the works of Bouts the elder and with those of Hans Memling.

In 1491-1492, Massys's name can be found in the registers of the Guild of St Luke in Antwerp. From what we know from the archives, he seems never again to have left Antwerp for any substantial period of time, though the possibility that he may have travelled to Italy or to France cannot be excluded. His first wife was Alyt Van Tuylt, by whom he had two children, Pauwel and Catharina. After her death, he remarried one Catharina Heyns, by whom he had ten children, the two eldest of whom, Jan and Cornelius, were to become painters in their turn. They were doubtless apprenticed to their father, and their uncle Jan also seems to have worked in his brother's studio. Quentin Massys was a famous and much-praised artist, who was able to live very comfortably. Many of his most illustrious contemporaries, including Erasmus and Sir Thomas More (the author of *Utopia*), held him to be an artist of the first order. It is also known that Dürer paid him a visit while he was staying in Antwerp, in 1520-1521.

*Above*

QUENTIN MASSYS
*The St Anne Altarpiece*
Left wing, *The Angel Speaks to Joachim.*
Musée d'Art ancien, Brussels.

*Opposite*

QUENTIN MASSYS
*Portrait of an Old Man*
C. 1517, oil on wood,
48 × 37 cm (19 × 14 1/2 in).
Musée Jacquemart-André, Paris.

# QUENTIN METSYS

QUENTIN MASSYS
*St Anne Altarpiece*
Detail of central panel,
*The Holy Kinship.*
Musée d'Art ancien, Brussels.

Our knowledge of his youthful œuvre depends largely upon conjecture. There are ten or so paintings, most of them *Madonnas*, that are candidates for attribution to the young Massys. But his first dated work is the *The Holy Kinship*, also known as *The St Anne Altarpiece*, now in Brussels. This triptych dates from 1507-1508, and was commissioned by the Confraternity of St Anne for their chapel in St Peter's church in Louvain. It is visibly the work of an experienced artist. The central panel shows the Virgin, the Holy Child and St Anne, with Mary the mother of James and Mary Salome sitting in the foreground with their children. Further back, there are four men standing behind the central figures, and behind them is an architectural fantasy in the Italian style, executed in trompe-l'œil. The overall effect is of a portrait of a rich, dignified middle-class family, with its severe patriarchs and its amiable and graceful women – a family such as one might meet among the newly-wealthy classes that had begun to proliferate in Antwerp, thanks to the development of the port, which in those days had recently established itself as the first in Europe.

On one of the wings, an angel with large wings outspread, brings the news that St Anne is with child to Joachim, as he kneels beside a rock, his hands raised in adoration. The other wing shows St Anne on her death bed, covered with a red sheet, her face pale, her mouth half-open, as if she had just breathed her last. Mary Salome, who has collapsed with grief, wipes the tears from her cheeks. The backs of the wings, when the triptych is closed, juxtapose two scenes. The first takes place beneath the portico of a church, the double arch of which gives onto a square, at the far end of which can be seen the tower of Antwerp cathedral. Under the portico, the High Priest of Jerusalem is receiving an ebony casket from St Anne, who lowers her eyes. Behind her, Joachim holds a parchment which contains the act of donation to the temple and its ministers. In the distance are two figures seen from behind: these too are Anne and Joachim, distributing money to the poor. In the second scene, Joachim's face and attitude express his distress and confusion: the High Priest has refused the coins Joachim has just placed on the offering table, and is gesturing to him brusquely to leave.

Massys may sometimes tend towards mawkishness in his treatment of these themes, but St Anne was a particularly popular legend in Flanders and Holland, and this painting brought him immediate and considerable success.

Massys is also famous for another triptych, *The Entombment*, or *St John Altarpiece*, now in the Antwerp museum. This is an almost oriental fantasy. Some of the figures were probably inspired by the many exotic faces the painter would have seen around him in Antwerp. The central panel depicts the moment

QUENTIN MASSYS
*St Anne Altarpiece*
Detail of right wing.
*The Death of St Anne.*
Musée d'Art ancien, Brussels.

at which Joseph of Arimathea comes to ask the Virgin for her permission to bury Christ's body. Mary, supported by John, is slipping down onto her knees. In the foreground, Joseph is picking small scraps of bloody flesh from Christ's head, while Nicodemus tries to lift up the corpse by its armpits. Behind them, a centurion is holding the crown of thorns in a piece of cloth, so as to protect his fingers. Mary Salome is preparing to anoint the wounds in Jesus's hands with a sponge passed to her by another woman. A little further back on the right are three smaller figures who are preparing the tomb. Far off to the left, we can see Jerusalem, and behind it, blue mountains fading away into an azure sky. Behind the central action is the hill of Golgotha, with its few trees, the cross and the crucified thieves, all of them represented on a much smaller scale in comparison with the foreground figures. A man is carrying a ladder across the hill, while two women busy

themselves mopping up the holy blood. They are watched as they work by two dogs and an owl.

The right hand panel is a scene of extraordinary cruelty, depicting St John, his body plunged into a cauldron of boiling oil. The saint, who is naked from the waist up, seems almost angelic, as if he were not suffering. Around him is a crowd of sadistic faces, ugly boors in garish clothes. The one exception to this rule is the figure of a young Flemish boy, who is watching the scene from above in a tree. The left wing shows Salome offering the head of St John the Baptist to Herod. In this panel every face bears the stamp of evil. Herodias uses the tip of her knife to make her mark in the saint's forehead; she is presented as the perfect courtisan, untrustworthy and vindictive. Herod himself, with his thick lips, hooked nose and narrowed eyes, even seems a little frightened by what he has just done. The whole panel is marked by an

QUENTIN MASSYS
*St John Altarpiece
(The Entombment)*
1507-1508, oil on wood,
260 × 504 cm (102 1/2 × 198 1/2 in).
Koninklijk Museum
voor Schone Kunsten, Antwerp.

QUENTIN MASSYS
*St Anne Altarpiece* (closed)
1509, oil on wood,
each panel 224.5 × 219 cm
(88 1/2 × 86 in).
Musée d'Art ancien, Brussels.

*Opposite*

QUENTIN MASSYS
*The Virgin Enthroned*
C. 1525, oil on wood,
135 × 90 cm (53 × 35 1/2 in).
Staatliche Museen, Berlin.

extraordinary sense of profane pleasure in such a sumptuous display of rich colours.

Massys's religious paintings are not as highly-rated today as they were during the artist's lifetime. The affectation and sentimentality that for many years guaranteed their popularity are now held against them. Some feel that Massys had fallen too much under the spell of da Vinci, as in his *Virgin*, which is clearly copied from Leonardo's *St Anne* ; others, that his *Temptation of St Anthony* lapses into a facile eroticism, preoccupied with the sensuous forms both of the women and of the saint himself, and does not bear comparison with Bosch's treatment of the same theme. Likewise, the painter's exaggeration of sentiment in the *Virgin Enthroned* in Berlin is now felt to lie beyond the bounds of good taste. Doubtless for reasons such as these, Massys's most popular painting today is *The Money Changer and His Wife*, in the Louvre.

This work belongs to the second group of paintings that make up Massys's œuvre. Massys did not work only for religious confraternities. He also painted portraits and other profane subjects, sometimes satirical, in response to commissions from humanists and scholars. He was perfectly attuned to the new

*Opposite, above*
QUENTIN MASSYS
*The Money Changer and His Wife*
1514, oil on wood, 74 × 68 cm (29 × 227 in).
Musée du Louvre, Paris

*Below*
*The Money Changer and His Wife*
Detail.

mercantile conception of art. Antwerp was already established as an active and liberal centre for trade in art, particularly during the annual fairs held at Easter and on St Bavo's feast-day, each of which lasted a full six weeks. During these fairs, artists and dealers from Antwerp and other Flemish towns would offer their works for sale on trestles and in booths, which were rented by their surface area. Not only painters and sculptors, but also the carpenters who made the panels on which the artists worked and who constructed the delicate articulated supports used for triptychs, would take part in these events. We cannot be certain that Massys sold his works on these occasions, but we do know that

he worked with one of the specialists in such markets, Joachim Patinir, who painted the landscapes for several of his pictures.

*The Money Changer and His Wife* was painted in 1514. It consists of two portraits, which the artist treats as a single genre scene. The activity of the couple adds interest and focus to the composition. Husband and wife are shown as half-length figures. They are leaning on a table, on which are placed coins, a circular mirror, and various other tokens of their wealth. Behind them are shelves filled with books and writing instruments, treated as a still life. The circular mirror, whether convex or not, is a frequent feature of Flemish art: we have seen it playing different roles

QUENTIN MASSYS
*The Ugly Duchess*
C. 1525-1530, oil on wood,
64 × 45.5 cm (25 × 18 in).
National Gallery, London.

in, amongst others, *The Arnolfini Marriage* by Jan Van Eyck and the *Saint Eligius* of Petrus Christus. Here it is used to provide an oblique reflection of a side window, under which we can just make out the tiny figure of a thief. He would seem to be spying on the couple as they count their gold, while they would seem to be oblivious to his presence, blinded by their greed.

Massys is one of the most important portraitists of the age, thanks above all to his pictures of Erasmus and Pierre Gilles (Petrus Aegidius), the town clerk of Antwerp, which he painted in 1517 and sent as a gift to Thomas More. The *Portrait of an Old Man* is an historically important work, for it is the first portrait by a Flemish artist to show the sitter in profile, following the Italian model. Massys's most astonishing work in this genre is certainly the *Grotesque Old Woman*, in the National Gallery in London. (This picture is also known as *The Ugly Duchess*, because Sir John Tenniel was later to use it in his illustrations for *Alice in Wonderland*.) Massys based his own picture on a caricature by Leonardo da Vinci. He was also influenced, according to Panofsky, by his friend Erasmus's book *In Praise of Folly*, in which the author describes old mad women who "still play the coquette", "cannot tear themselves away from their mirrors", and "do not hesitate to exhibit their repulsive withered breasts". The effects of the huge ears, wrinkles, and ape-like face, are merely emphasized by the ridiculous hat. The sitter is made even more repugnant by the rich jewels she wears and the indiscretion of her low-cut dress. This picture is a prodigious exercise in the grotesque, in which Massys proves himself not only an astute critic of human vanity, but a worthy precursor of Goya and Picasso.

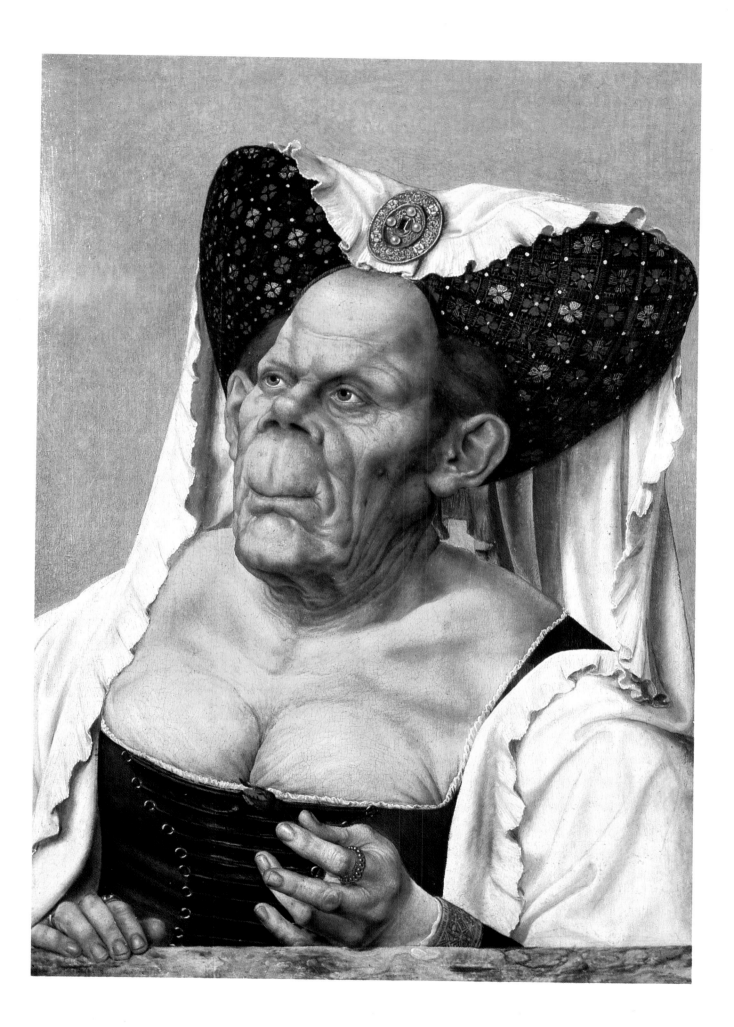

# IN THE SHADOW
# OF THE MASTERS

Throughout this century of perpetual innovation, the great creative figures of Flemish painting were surrounded by many "minor" artists. These lesser-known painters have often been treated with condescension, merely because they happened to be overshadowed by the major creators. But many of them are no less remarkable on that account.

Among these secondary figures, certain names stand out, such as those of Jacques Daret, the talented figure painter, and Gérard David, the faithful guardian of the Flemish tradition. Some of the finest work was also produced by anonymous hands, painters such as the Master of the Legend of St Ursula, and the Master of the Adoration of Khanenko. In their day, these painters were widely celebrated for their achievements. Meanwhile the great portraitist, Jan Gossart, a contemporary of Quentin Massys, introduced the neo-classicical nude and its attendant mythology as subjects in their own right. With Massys, Gossart was one of those responsible for the emergence of genre painting.

GÉRARD DAVID
*The Marriage at Cana*
Detail, *The Virgin.*
Musée du Louvre, Paris.

# THE LESSER MASTERS

## JACQUES DARET

Jacques Daret was born at Tournai in around 1403, and, save for a few brief interludes, spent the rest of his life in the city of his birth. He was trained in Robert Campin's studio, where he spent fifteen years or so, before setting up as a master in his own right. Without being a genius in the strict sense of the term, he was yet an excellent artist with a thorough grasp of the techniques of his trade. In many ways, he was quite the equal of his more famous contemporaries, and was above all a supremely talented draughtsman. He was one of the stars of the Burgundian court, and was twice chosen in preference to all competitors when Philip the Good and Charles the Bold were looking for someone to organize a ceremonial occasion. His principal patron over a period of twenty years was the abbot of St Vaart, Jean de Clercq.

The numerous works that Jacques Daret produced for the abbot provide an ideal illustration of the range of activity typical of a 15th-century painter. Between 1433 and 1436, Daret painted five polychrome statues for the abbot's funerary monument. He painted the panels for an altarpiece dedicated to the Virgin, as well as colouring the polychrome sculptures and making a protective glass frame in which to enclose the whole to keep it free of dust and dirt. He also painted a series of portraits representing the different abbots of the abbey since its foundation by Theodoric III, King of the Franks. Daret was also a master of the art of illumination. On 8 May 1436, one Éleuthère du Pret engaged him "to teach him the art of illumination[1]". Yet, out of all of Daret's works that are recorded in Jean de Clercq's account books,

1. *Cf.* Jellie Dijkstra, *op. cit.*, p. 332.

*Above*

JACQUES DARET
*Altarpiece of the Virgin*
Detail of the panel, *The Presentation in the Temple.*

*Opposite*

*Altarpiece of the Virgin*
Panel, *The Presentation in the Temple.*
1433-1435, oil on wood,
57.5 × 52 cm (22 1/2 × 20 1/2 in).
Musée du Petit Palais, Paris.

only four panels have survived to the present day. They come from an *Altarpiece of the Virgin* painted for the abbot between 1433 and 1435. Two of them, the *Visitation* and the *Adoration of the Magi*, are in the State Collections in Berlin; the third, the *Nativity*, is in the Thyssen-Bornemisza collection, and the fourth, the *Presentation in the Temple*, is in the Petit Palais museum, in Paris.

One of these four panels, *The Visitation* is reminiscent in its composition of paintings by Rogier Van der Weyden on the same theme. But the three others are closer — strikingly close — to the art of Robert Campin, especially *the Nativity* which should be compared with Campin's *Nativity* in Dijon. The two compositions are essentially analogous: the Virgin kneels before the Infant who is lying on the ground, while Joseph holds up a lighted candle. They also share the small group of angels and the scene of the two midwives taken from an apocryphal Gospel, which Daret treats as a separate episode. Daret is less inventive than Campin, and his ambition seems limited to creating a simple tranquil atmosphere. The clothes worn by the midwives are less exotic, and the angels are holding a single phylactery. Above all, Daret's *Nativity* has been substantially simplified: it has fewer characters, and materials and textures are rendered with less attention than in Campin's. One has only to look at the ageing skeleton of the stable to measure the distance that separates the two artists. Certain elements have also been modified, so that, for instance, the ass and the ox in Daret's picture face towards the scene of the Birth, rather than turning their backs on it.

The other three panels show that Daret was a talented painter of the human figure and a sensitive landscape artist. Unfortunately, all his later work has been either lost or destroyed, and we thus know nothing of how the young painter's career developed after this altarpiece.

## Gérard David

Gérard David's career began some fifty years later than that of Jacques Daret. Today, David is known essentially as a painter of religious subjects and justice scenes. He was made a master of the Bruges corporation of picture makers and saddlers on 14 January 1484. He swiftly achieved fame, fortune and social status. From 1494 to his death, he worked in a studio opposite the Vlamijnckbrugghe. Perhaps in the hope of acquiring a wider market for this work, he also joined the Antwerp guild of painters

in 1515. However, there is no evidence that he ever lived in Antwerp. He seems to have been prone to quarrelling. In 1520, following an argument with one of his former companions over a chest containing models and sketches, he was sentenced to several months in prison. But despite his irascible temper, David was also noted for his charitable generosity, and he was closely connected with the Carmelite convent at Sion. We do not know the exact extent of his œuvre as a painter, but it seems to have been considerable. He was buried beneath the towers of the church of Notre Dame in Bruges.

David's first paintings probably date from the years between 1480 and 1484. They reflect a Dutch influence in his early training. Soon after he arrived in Bruges, however, in 1487 and 1488, the municipal authorities requested him to paint a series of panels for the deputy burgomaster's room in the town hall. This major commission took the form of a large diptych that was first mentioned in the city archives as a *Last Judgement*, but which in fact depicts *The Judgement of Cambyses*. The subject is taken from Herodotus: the judge Sisamnes, who had been guilty of prevarication, was arrested and punished by Cambyses, the King of Persia. For his crimes, Sisamnes was condemned to be flayed alive. David represents this scene with a cold and exemplary cruelty. Like the paintings Dieric Bouts made for the town hall in Louvain, David's panels were intended as a stern warning to judges against the temptation of corruption.

David's art reached its full maturity during the period between 1500 and 1515. During this time he was commissioned to paint several large-scale works. Changes in his style are clearly visible in the *Baptism of Christ* triptych which he produced for Jan de Trompes, the bailiff of Ostende and chief tax collector of Flanders. The baptism is depicted in the midst of a vast verdant

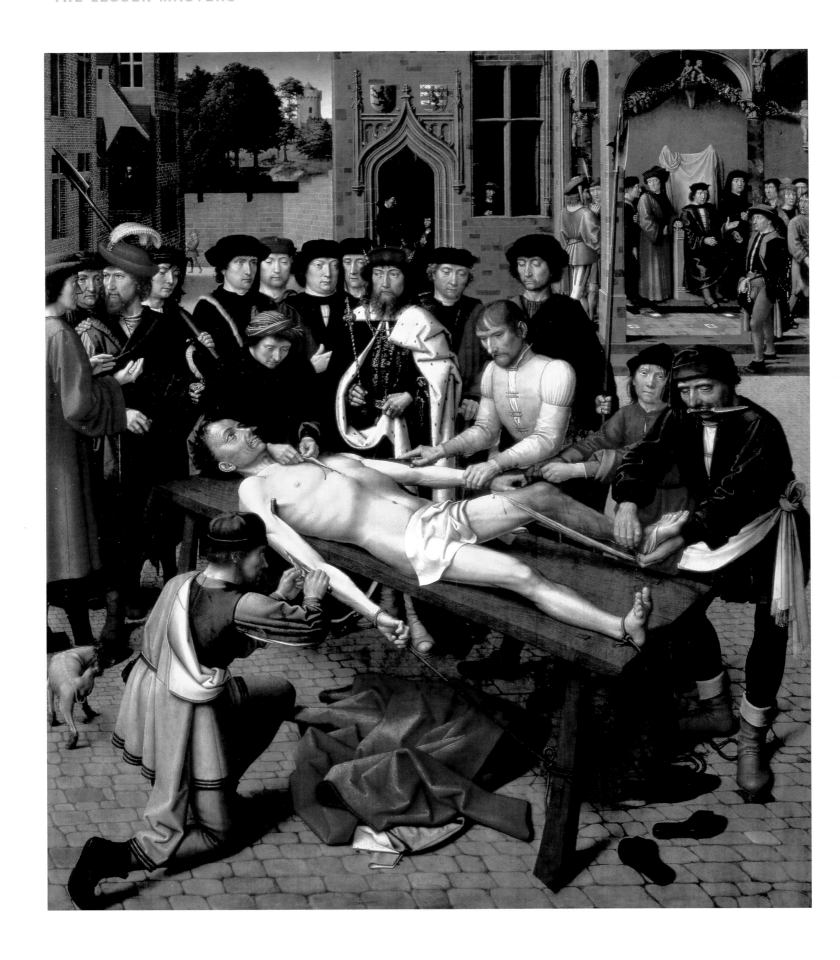

landscape. David's cold palette here contrasts with the harsh light that characterized his early work. The whole work, in fact, clearly demonstrates the profound influence of Jan Van Eyck's style and technique. The image of God the Father hovering encircled by clouds, and the wingless angel with red hair holding Christ's robe, are borrowed directly from the *Adoration of the Lamb* altarpiece in St Bavo's Cathedral, Ghent. The clearly-defined foliage in the foreground, and the meticulous rendering of materials, especially the crude weaving of John the Baptist's tunic, are all signs of David's desire to imitate, or even surpass, the admirably precise style of the Van Eyck brothers.

His late period stretches from 1515 to his death in 1523 and during that time he painted several different surviving versions of the *Rest on the Flight into Egypt.* These paintings are very gentle in mood, and the palette creates an exquisite harmony of different blues. This dominant blue tonality and the delicate treatment of form are characteristic of David's late style. David also invented a composition that was to influence artists throughout the 16th century: the Virgin and Child, with or without Joseph, seated in the centre of a huge landscape, and surrounded by objects such as a basket or a gourd, the presence of which defines the theme.

Gérard David's œuvre was extremely diverse, judging by the forty or so paintings now attributed to him, and over the course of his career, his style often underwent modifications. He was apparently torn between a modernizing tendancy, and the still vigorous traditions of Burgundian Flanders. David displayed a gift for innovation in his use of landscape and in his approach to iconography, yet all his motifs, and all his sources of inspiration, can be traced back to the great artists of the preceding decades. Jan Van Eyck, above all, was – for David – an absolute master, in whom his faith never wavered. He clearly considered his practice of copying these former masters to be an integral part of his own creative process. From them, David's painting took not only much of its magnificence, but also an undimmed pride in tradition.

MASTER OF THE LEGEND OF ST URSULA
*Scenes from the Life of St Ursula*
Detail, *The Massacre by the Huns.*
Groeninge Museum, Bruges.

# THE MASTER OF THE LEGEND OF ST URSULA

In 1903, the famous art historian J.M. Friedländer attributed the *Scenes from the Life of St Ursula*, today in the Groeninge Museum, to a painter he called The Master of the Legend of St Ursula. He saw this artist as a particularly talented disciple of Memling and Rogier Van der Weyden. In 1921, another historian, Martin Conway, proposed that this anonymous artist was one Pieter Casembroot, a painter from Bruges who had been apprenticed to Arnout de Mol, before becoming a master himself in 1459, none of whose works had hitherto been identified. Today, this hypothesis is widely accepted. Casembroot's most productive years were those between 1480 and 1500. We also know that, in around 1480, he began to receive so many commissions that he had to follow the example of his more illustrious colleagues and set up a studio in his own name.

Before arriving in the Groeninge Museum, the *Polyptych of St Ursula* seems never to have left the Benedictine convent in Bruges. Documentary evidence suggests the painting was executed between January 1474 and August 1475. These dates would seem to be confirmed by the fact that the Bruges belfry appears in several of the panels without its celebrated octagonal top, which was only added in 1483. This polyptych would therefore predate Hans Memling's St Ursula shrine of 1489. If that is indeed the case, then it is the work of a great innovator. Free of the influence of existing models, Casembroot invented a highly personal manner of retelling the saint's legend, especially in the panel showing the departure of the eleven thousand virgins.

The same skill is evident in the *Portrait of Ludovico Portinari,* now in Philadelphia. The artist is a master of the human face, and this magnificent work abounds in life and presence. He uses grey shadow to render the merest facial line, creating a superb relief effect. The great, dark, almost protruding eyes, and the ear with its helix elongated like a scythe, are characteristic of the painter's style. Portinari's hands are energetic, long and firm, and they too are rendered using a marvellous pattern of shadowing which creates an effect of intense life. Despite a certain aristocratic appearance, their strength is reminiscent of the energy which Hugo Van der Goes imparted to the hands of his peasants.

This portrait was originally part of a diptych on the theme of the *Virgin and Child with Angels*, and was probably painted in 1479. Once again, the date is supported by the unfinished belfry in the background, which has still to receive its octagonal crown of 1483. This work thus predates Memling's *Martin Van*

THE MASTER
OF THE KHANENKO ADORATION
*Triptych The Adoration
of the Magi*
Oil on wood, 29 × 39 cm
(14 1/2 × 15 3/8 in).
Musée des Beaux-Arts,
Saint-Omer.

*Nieuwenhove Diptych* of 1487. It is therefore possible, not only that the Master of the Legend of St Ursula was a painter of great talent in his own right, but that he was twice able to impose a model he had invented on his rival Memling.

# Jan Gossart

Jan Gossart was a painter, draughtsman and engraver. He was born in 1478, most probably in the Burgundian province of Hainaut. It was under the name "Jennyn Van Henegouwe" (John of Hainaut) that he was received as a master of the Guild of St Luke at Antwerp in 1503. We do not know where he was apprenticed, and his early career is largely obscure. The composition and nature of certain of his religious paintings suggest he may have trained in Bruges, perhaps with Gérard David. But he also seem to have been one of the first representatives of what we may call Antwerp mannerism, as can be seen in his signed drawing, *The Mystic Marriage of St Catherine*.

In 1508, Gossart travelled with Philip of Burgundy, the admiral of Zeeland, whom Margaret of Austria had sent to Rome as her envoy to Pope Julius II. They interrupted their journey to visit Trento, Verona, Mantua and Florence, where Gossart discovered the luminous art of the Quattrocento, and the splendours of classical Antiquity. On his return, he continued to study and paint for several years (1509-1516), without being able to make full use of his Italian discoveries. During this period, he received many commissions on religious subjects, for which he drew on the iconographical and technical resources of the Flemish tradition, the inventions of the Italian renaissance, and the inspirational example of Dürer. His *Christ in the Garden of Olives* is one of the first northern nocturnes, and its violent intensity owes something to both Dürer and Mantegna.

When he moved to Souburg at the end of 1515, Gossart finally found the place where he could express himself as an artist of the Renaissance and fully exploit his experience in Rome. There he was encouraged by the prince and humanist Philip of Burgundy, who drew him into his plan to construct an Italian-style palace decorated with figures from classical mythology. It was thus that Gossart came to paint life-size secular nudes, a subject for which there was no precedent in the former provinces of Burgundian Flanders. As Guicciardini was to say, in 1567: "John of Hainaut was the first to bring the art of representing historical and poetical subjects with nude figures from Italy to the countries of the North." The following year, Gossart, following Philip of Burgundy's instructions, decorated Ferdinand the Catholic's funeral hearse with nude figures and martial trophies in the classical vein. And later, in 1527, he painted one final work on a mythological subject, a large-scale work, using sober and elegant architectural motifs as the setting for its subject.

Gossart always devoted much of his time to drawing. He was particularly attracted to pen and ink drawing, more so

JAN GOSSART
*Danaë*
Alte Pinakothek, Munich.

than to drawing in pencil. His œuvre includes many projects for engravings, paintings and stained glass windows. Dürer was always his master in this domain, and it was apparently Dürer's stay in the Netherlands in 1520 and the consequent diffusion of his prints, that inspired Gossart to make his only engravings: two with burin, one etching and two woodblock prints.

Gossart also painted many portraits. By their rigourous psychological analysis he is surely one of the most talented nothern artists to have practised this genre. His finest works in this respect are probably the *Man with Rosary* and *The Old Couple*, in the National Gallery, London, along with *The Children of Christian II of Denmark*. Usually, he would paint his sitters against a dark background. After 1525, he began to use a slab of coloured marble as backdrop, and provide a trompe-l'œil frame of the kind that can be seen in certain Florentine portraits.

Gossart's art was intensely personal and innovative. Although it had virtually no impact on his contemporaries, it was to profoundly influence the subsequent generation of painters. After his death in 1532, his fame began to spread through Italy, and during the 17th and 18th centuries he was also considered a major artist in the Southern Netherlands, despite the many transformations that the art of the North was about to undergo.

IOANNES, MALBODIVS, PINGEBAT, 1527,

Ainsworth, Maryen W. and Martens, Maximiliann P.J., *Petrus Christus*, Paris, 1995.

Bosque, A. de, *Quentin Metsys*, Brussels, 1975.

*Les Primitifs flamands et leur temps*, Louvain-La-Neuve, 1994.

Comblen-Sonkes, M. and Vronee-Verhaegen, N., *Les Primitifs flamands, le musée des Beaux-Arts de Dijon*, 2 volumes, Brussels, 1987.

Delanda, O., *Rogier Van der Weyden*, Paris, 1987.

De Vos, D., *Hans Memling: The Complete Works*, London, 1994.

Dhanens, E., *Hubert and Jan Van Eyck*, New York, n.d.

Fromentin, E., *The Masters of Past Time*, London, 1941.

Houtard, M., *Jacques Daret, peintre tournaisien du XVᵉ siècle*, Tournai, 1908.

Marijnissen, R.H., et Ruyffelaen, P., *Bosch*, Antwerp, 1987.

Michel, É., *La Peinture au musée du Louvre, école flamande*, Paris, 1944.

Panofsky, E., *Early Netherlandish Painting: Its Origins and Character*, Cambridge, MA, 1953.

Ségard, A., *Jean Gossart dit Mabuse*, Brussels, 1923.

Tolnay, Ch. de, *Le Maître de Flémalle et les frères Van Eyck*, Brussels, 1939.

Van Puyvelde, L., *Les Primitifs flamands, musée de l'Orangerie*, Paris, 1947.

Wauters, A.J., *La Peinture flamande*, Paris, 1896.

Wauters, A.J., *Hugues Van der Goes, sa vie, son œuvre*, Brussels, 1872.

*Left*
ROGIER VAN DER WEYDEN
**Portrait of Jean I, Duke of Clèves**
1468, oil on wood,
49.5 × 31.5 cm (19 1/2 × 12 1/2 in).
Musée du Louvre, Paris.

*Right*
HANS MEMLING
**Portrait of an Old Woman.**
Musée du Louvre, Paris.

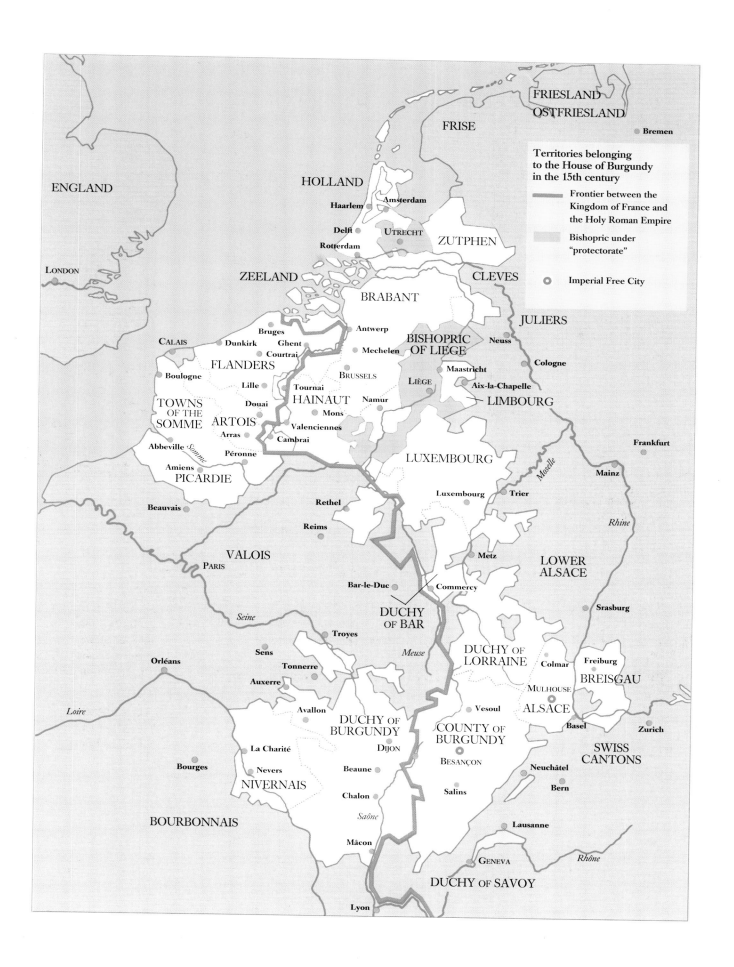

FRIESLAND
OSTFRIESLAND
FRISE
Bremen

ENGLAND
HOLLAND
Haarlem  Amsterdam
Delft  UTRECHT
Rotterdam  ZUTPHEN
CLEVES

LONDON
ZEELAND
BRABANT
JULIERS
Bruges  Antwerp  BISHOPRIC  Neuss
CALAIS  Dunkirk  Ghent  Mechelen  OF LIÈGE
FLANDERS  Courtrai  Liège  Cologne
Boulogne  BRUSSELS  Maastricht
Lille  Tournai  Namur  Aix-la-Chapelle
TOWNS  Douai  HAINAUT  LIMBOURG
OF THE  ARTOIS  Mons  LUXEMBOURG
SOMME  Valenciennes  Frankfurt
Abbeville  Arras  Cambrai  Mainz
Somme  Péronne  Rethel  Luxembourg  Trier
Amiens  Reims  Moselle
PICARDIE  Rhine
Beauvais  LOWER
VALOIS  Metz  ALSACE
PARIS  Srasburg
Bar-le-Duc  Commercy
Seine  DUCHY  DUCHY OF  Colmar  Freiburg
OF BAR  LORRAINE  BREISGAU
Troyes  Meuse  MULHOUSE
Orléans  Sens  DUCHY OF  ALSACE
Tonnerre  LORRAINE  Basel  Zurich
Auxerre  Vesoul  SWISS
Loire  Avallon  COUNTY OF  CANTONS
DUCHY OF  BURGUNDY  Neuchâtel
Bourges  BURGUNDY  DIJON  Besançon  Bern
La Charité  Beaune  Salins
Nevers  Lausanne
NIVERNAIS  Chalon
BOURBONNAIS  Saône  Rhône
Mâcon  Geneva
Lyon  DUCHY OF SAVOY

Territories belonging
to the House of Burgundy
in the 15th century

Frontier between the
Kingdom of France and
the Holy Roman Empire

Bishopric under
"protectorate"

○ Imperial Free City

PHOTOGRAPHIC CREDITS

Agence Bulloz, Paris: p. 49, 51, 62, 63, 174, 176, 192, 193, 202, 205. Agence Giraudon, Paris: p. 12, 16 (right), 19, 20, 24, 25, 26, 27, 28, 29, 30, 31, 32-33, 34, 35, 36, 37, 38, 48, 59, 64, 65, 66, 67, 72-73, (79), 80, 94, 97, 100, 101, 102, 103, 107, 108-109, 120, 121, 122, 123, 124, 139, 140, 141, 144, 145, 148-149, 150, 151, 166, 167, 168, 169, 175, 177, 178-179, 180, 184, 189, 196, 197. Agence RMN, Paris: p. 40-41, 113, 114, 142-143, 190, 195, 199, 206 (right). Artothek, Munich: p. 52, 54, 81, 82, 110-111. Staatliche Museen zu Berlin, Bildarchiv Preussischer Kulturbesitz, Berlin: p. 47, 87, 125, 126, 185 and cover. Courtauld Institute Galleries, London: p. 55, 56-57. Erich Lessing, Vienna: p. 2, 6, 8, 9, 10, 11, 14, 15, 16 (left), 17, 18, 22, 39, 68, 69, 71, 74, 75, 76-77, 104, 105, 106, 112, 115, 116, 117, 119, 128-129, 130, 131, 133, 136, 138, 146, 147, 152, 153, 154-155, 156-157, 159, 160, 161, 162, 163, 164-165, 170, 171, 172, 173, 186-187, 206 (left). Fundacion Coleccion Thyssen-Bornemisza, Madrid: p. 93. Groeninge Museum, Bruges: p. 46, 134, 201. Koninklijk Museum voor Schone Kunsten, Antwerp: p. 182-183. Kunsthistorisches Museum, Vienna: p. 45, 135. Metropolitan Museum of Art, New York: p. 60, 61 (The Cloisters collection), 84, 89 (Robert Lehman collection, 1905). Musée royal des Beaux-Arts de Belgique, Brussels: p. 85, 90-91. National Gallery of Art, Washington: p. 5. The National Gallery, London: p. 96, 98. The Nelson-Atkins Museum of Art, Kansas City: p. 92. Ursula Edelmann, Frankfurt: p. 53.

Printed in Italy
by OFFSET PRINT VENETA
Verona